MotoGP
Season Guide 2005

Julian Ryder *Foreword by* **Suzi Perry**

official **motogp**
licensed product

First published in March 2005

A catalogue record for this book is available from the British Library

ISBN 1 84425 134 9

Library of Congress catalog card no. 2004117155

Haynes Publishing, Sparkford, Yeovil, Somerset BA22 7JJ, UK
Tel: +44 (0) 1963 442030
Fax: +44 (0) 1963 440001
E-mail: sales@haynes.co.uk
Website: www.haynes.co.uk

Haynes North America, Inc.,
861 Lawrence Drive, Newbury Park,
California 91320, USA

Printed and bound by J.H.Haynes & Co Ltd, Sparkford, Yeovil, Somerset BA22 7JJ, UK

This product is officially licensed by Dorna SL, owners of the MotoGP trademark
(© Dorna 2005)

Managing Editor Louise McIntyre
Design Lee Parsons, Paul Bullock (Maluma)
Sub-editor Kay Edge
Advertising Sales David Dew (Motocom)
Photography Malcolm Bryan/BPC, Gold & Goose

Author's Acknowledgements
This book is for my wife Wendy who, after mature reflection, decided not to divorce me when I was away at the IRTA Barcelona tests on our tenth wedding anniversary.

Help with photography was provided by Malcolm Bryan, David Goldman, Peter Fox, Richens/LAT, and Andrew Northcott. Haynes' designer Lee Parsons felt forced to listen to some of their advice while assembling this book in the Barcelona circuit's press room against a tight deadline.

Dr Martin Raines, supplier of statistics to Dorna, performed his usual magic with a database.

At Dorna, Nick Harris, Eva Jirsenska and Phaedra Haramis did their best to expedite matters.

As usual paddock people in both the press room and the teams went out of their way to help. Thank you everybody.

UP FRONT

RACES

CONTENTS

BIKES AND RIDERS

TAIL ENDERS

SUZI PERRY
FOREWORD

Suzi will again be presenting the BBC's coverage of MotoGP during the 2005 season, while keeping one eye on the Wolverhampton Wanderers' score

Valentino Rossi. Are there two more powerful or apt words with which to begin this book? I don't think so. His achievements last season prove the point perfectly. To win championships back to back, with different manufacturers, speaks volumes. And history took a long time to repeat itself. Fifteen years separated Eddie Lawson's Yamaha/Honda victories from Rossi's reverse switch, but there was one big difference – the young Italian did it for fun! One of my favourite images from last year was seeing the tears of disbelief run down Vale's cheek in Welkom, after he had taken the first win. The 2004 season was special and we knew it would be, but what about this season?

During the winter months there have been various changes in the paddock, with riders moving teams and the inevitable technical advances from the factories. Personally, I'm looking forward to seeing how the mighty HRC deal with their humiliating defeat in '04. They now have Max Biaggi and Nicky Hayden in the factory hot seats, but will that be enough to take on Doctor Rossi and the Texas Tornado, Colin Edwards? It's also Yamaha's 50th birthday and they won't be inviting Honda to spoil the party.

There will be new tracks for the riders to get their heads around, too. For the first time China and Turkey open their doors, and MotoGP also makes a welcome return to the USA, to the site of one of the world's greatest turns, the Corkscrew at Laguna Seca. I can already hear the sound of champagne corks popping...

This is a terrific era for bike racing: Rossi ensures that. However, he won't be in our midst for ever so drink it in while you can. As you watch the stories unfold, keep this guide handy. After all, we all want to be experts!

THERE ARE MORE QUESTIONS THAN ANSWERS
MotoGP 2005

There cannot have been many seasons in the entire history of Grand Prix motorcycle racing which have been more keenly anticipated than 2005. More races than ever before, in more countries than ever before, plus the welcome return to the USA and the adventure that will be the Chinese GP.

All the interest will, as usual, centre on Valentino Rossi. This year there will be seven Honda V5s ranged against him. Will a worthy challenger emerge from that pack on whom HRC can concentrate their efforts? Or will Suzuki and Kawasaki step up to the plate after their encouraging progress last year? Surely Ducati won't make the same mistakes again and will return to their winning ways. Will any of the young guns make the leap from occasional flashes of brilliance to full-on stardom? The Michelin versus Bridgestone tyre war looks likely to escalate, especially with Ducati.

This book is designed to help you follow a fascinating season. All the information you need is here: career details of every rider, statistics for every track (including maps with every gear change and the speed on every bend). If it rains you'll need to know about the new wet weather procedure, so check the Rules & Regulations section. In brief, riders will be allowed to change bikes if conditions warrant it but to prevent sharp practice they would have to go out on different tyres from those they came in on. Come in on slicks and you have to go out with treaded tyres and vice versa. The pitlane will be transpondered and a 60kph speed limit enforced. The most optimistic assessment is that changing bikes will cost you 30 or 40 seconds, quite enough to rule out pitting to change machine as a race tactic. The other major change is in fuel tank capacity; it comes down to 22 litres, a 2-litre reduction. Will that put a cap on performance? Lap records have tumbled since the MotoGP formula arrived in 2002, so if that trend is reversed you'll know fuel economy is becoming a factor.

The other major change is to MotoGP qualifying. Only the Saturday afternoon session will count for the grid. The other three sessions are just practice. The 125 and 250 classes are sticking with the old system whereby grid positions are decided counting times from both the Friday and Saturday afternoon sessions.

Will any one rider come out of the pack to challenge the all-conquering Rossi? Many pundits think Makoto Tamada is the most likely candidate

MotoGP SCHEDULE

FRIDAY

09.00 – 09.45	125cc	Free Practice 1
10.00 – 11.00	MotoGP	Free Pracice 1
11.15 – 12.15	250cc	Free Practice 1
13.15 – 13.45	125cc	Qualifying Practice 1
14.00 – 15.00	MotoGP	Qualifying Practice 1
15.15 – 16.00	250cc	Qualifying Practice 1

SATURDAY

09.00 – 09.45	125cc	Free Practice 2
10.00 – 11.00	MotoGP	Free Pracice 2
11.15 – 12.15	250cc	Free Practice 2
13.15 – 13.45	125cc	Qualifying Practice 2
14.00 – 15.00	MotoGP	Qualifying Practice 2
15.15 – 16.00	250cc	Qualifying Practice 2

SUNDAY

08.45 – 09.05	125cc	Warm Up
09.15 – 09.35	250cc	Warm Up
09.45 – 10.05	MotoGP	Warm Up
11.00	125cc	**RACE**
12.15	250cc	**RACE**
14.00	MotoGP	**RACE**

Whatever happens, don't watch the telly without this book.

Many paddock people helped me assemble the facts and figures on these pages, for which many thanks. The Suzuki MotoGP Team supplied us with the track data direct from their on-board data recording; Yamaha supplied most of the information on bike set-up – and you can read updated and extended versions on www.yamaha-racing.com before every race. The ever-wonderful Suzi Perry again wrote the foreword, and it's good to see the Beeb adding an extra half-hour to their MotoGP coverage plus some qualifying sessions on interactive services. British Eurosport will again provide their comprehensive coverage of all classes for the more committed petrol heads among you. It's nice to be able to report that viewing figures are up for MotoGP worldwide and that crowds at the circuits are also growing.

We're watching an exceptional era of motorcycle racing: enjoy it.

Julian Ryder

Evolution in Action
A new breed of leathers from the UK's number one

Ask about the HG Club Card.
Interest-free credit available.

(call 0800 165 165 or apply in store)

CARD

6332 L567 1998 1059
VALID FROM   EXPIRES END
00/00   00/00
MR A N OTHER

Hein Gericke

HE STUNNING NEW HG CELTIC SUIT
ONE-PIECE £379.98
WO-PIECE: JACKET £199.99 PANTS £179.99

- Tailored racing fit
- 1.2 mm cowhide
- Perforated leather in the front (one-piece only)
- Pre-shaped sleeves and legs
- Racing back spoiler (one-piece only)
- Leather reinforcement at vulnerable areas
- Additional padding in selected places
- Generous stretch zones
- Skin-friendly removable mesh lining
- Practical inside pocket

- Knee sliders included
- SAFE® safety seams
- Hiprotec® V protectors on shoulders, elbows and knees
- Hiprotec® Backshock back protector
- Hiprotec® hip protectors retrofittable
- Reflective 3M Scotchlite® strips
- Colours: blk/wht/blu; blk/wht/grn; blk/wht/slv; blk/wht/yel; blk/wht/red
- One-piece sizes: 48-58
- Jacket & pants sizes: ladies 34-42; men's 48-58

ORDER HOTLINE 0800 165 165

Hein Gericke
For bike & body

hein-gericke.co.uk

eat, breathe, live MotoGP?

We know exactly how you feel, so are offering £5 off all these incredible MotoGP titles with free P&P! So whether you want to see the 2004 season again or find out about the amazing machinery these talented riders tame - don't miss out!

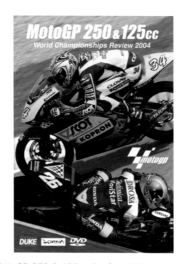

MotoGP Review 2004
Relive an awesome, knee-scraping season of racing as MotoGP Review 2004 brings you all the exciting highlights from practices and races, with an on-board lap from every circuit. Witness the thrills and spills as no spectator can, via on-bike and trackside cameras in this sensational review. A must-have for any MotoGP fan!
Was £19.99 NOW £14.99!
No.DMDVD1733 195mins

MotoGP 250 & 125cc Review 2004
All the very best action from the classes where the world's hottest up-and-coming stars prove themselves. Riders like Pedrosa in the 250cc and Dovizioso in the 125cc go all out to stake their claim on a ride in the premier league. Includes the sensational highlights from each and every one of the 16 rounds.
Was £19.99 NOW £14.99!
No.DMDVD1735 180mins

MotoGP The 210mph Bikes
What makes MotoGP bikes the fastest racing bikes in the world? Up to 230bhp has probably got something to do with it! In this all-new programme from Dorna, Randy Mamola unravels the technical wizardry behind the 7 MotoGP bikes: Honda, Yamaha, Ducati, Kawasaki, Aprilia, Suzuki and Proton.
Was £16.99 NOW £11.99!
No.DMDVD1648 80mins

To take advantage of these very special offers, all you need to do is ring 01624 640000 and quote Code No.3835

RACES

The where and when of all 17 rounds of the 2005 MotoGP Championship

On the following pages you'll find all the detail you need for complete enjoyment of MotoGP on TV. Make sure this book is open at the right page for easy reference when the coverage starts.

Thanks to the help of the Suzuki team, this year we are able to bring you details of gearchange points and corner speeds directly from their data logging system. I have rounded the speeds they supplied - to two decimal places - to the nearest 5mph or 5kmh so the figures are easier to assimilate.

Yamaha supplied the set-up information that you'll find under the Bikes heading. When a change is mentioned, as in a stiffer or softer spring, that means in relation to the base setting that riders and teams like to start with.

You will also find potted histories of each MotoGP race that has taken place at the track and a rider's view of the track and/or event. Go to a rider's page for more detail of a particular race.

The panel headed The Track is mainly for those of you contemplating going and watching at a venue. However, so you can recreate the correct atmosphere in your own living room I have suggested what you should eat and drink while watching TV. The research for that bit was fun.

motogp

SPANISH GP

ROUND **1**

JEREZ

10th April
CIRCUITO DE JEREZ
www.circuitodejerez.com

Valentino Rossi starts the
defence of his title at one of
his favourite circuits

There is no better way to start a new season than in Spain's deep south – Andalucia. Over 200,000 up-for-it local fans pack the stands to brew up the most intense atmosphere of the year. They are there to see national sporting heroes Gibernau, Elias and Pedrosa, figures as well-known in Spain as Beckham, Button and Kelly Holmes in the UK. However, even here the swathes of yellow demonstrate that, nowadays, every race is a home race for Valentino Rossi.

There are no fewer than three GPs in Spain, but

this is the one that actually carries the title 'Spanish GP'. Ironically, it's in the area most Spaniards would regard as least Spanish – certainly the inhabitants of Barcelona and Valencia, where the other two races take place, never mind the metropolitan sophisticates of Madrid. Happily, the area around Jerez de la Frontera and its Moorish-influenced cities, Cordoba, Granada and Seville, correspond to what a foreigner thinks Spain should be like – all ancient hilltop towns and cities dripping with history. Granada has the Alhambra, possibly the most beautiful complex of buildings in Europe, Cordoba the Mesquita, an amazing mosque-cum-cathedral, while Seville's enormous gothic cathedral contains the tomb of Columbus.

Circuito de Jerez

THE TRACK

Where is it?
Just outside Jerez, about six miles down the road to Arcos. You're unlikely to find a hotel room in either town so if you don't fancy camping go the other way towards the coast and Cadiz. Lots of the action now happens in Puerto de Santa Maria.

Is it worth going to?
Oh yes, if you can stand the pace. But remember, for your own safety, that in this part of the world Francis Drake is considered a pirate not a national hero.

How do I get tickets?
If you want a seat (and you do), buy before you travel from www.circuitodejerez.com

Where do I watch from?
There are grandstands all round the track and plenty of big screens to keep you in touch. The largest and rowdiest stands line the hillside around the Nieto and Peluqui corners – stands P, Q and W. Stands C, J and M between the first two corners also give you a panoramic view of the action.

Where does the overtaking happen?
The hardest braking effort is at Dry Sack. Turn 1 is also a favourite, as is the last bend, with the bonus that you get to see the plot unfolding through the massively fast right-handers that lead up to it.

TV times
One hour ahead of UK time.

What should you eat and drink while watching the TV?
The driest fino sherry you can find accompanied by a few pieces of chorizo (spicy paprika sausage) and maybe a slice of tortilla.

In the 2004 Spanish MotoGP Sete Gibernau reminded everyone that he is by far the best wet-weather rider on the grid

THE BIKES

Jerez looks like a Honda track and, since the inception of MotoGP, only one rostrum finisher has not been on a Honda. That's probably down to the circuit's all-round requirements. However, don't expect that to stop Rossi: it's one of his favourite tracks.

The quality of racing here is due to Jerez's undulating layout, plentiful hard braking efforts and countless camber changes. There are short, medium and long corners plus uphill and downhill braking. Chassis balance, especially during heavy braking, is therefore a major issue.

Front forks need to deal with high braking loads yet must also have enough movement left to ensure that it is their springs rather than the tyres which absorb those bumps on corner entries. Increasing the spring rate will prevent the front from diving too quickly under heavy deceleration. The fork's compression damping is set to allow enough high-speed movement to deal with the repetitive bumps, but rebound is dialled in to slow the fork's return travel to prevent understeer as the rider makes the transition from brakes to throttle and the weight transfers towards the rear. Rear spring rate will be set quite firm to prevent the bike squatting under power through the high-speed corners, while compression damping is lowered to help get drive off positively cambered turns.

MotoGP @ JEREZ

2004 Gibernau warmed the crowd up with a faultless performance in monsoon conditions – not an uncommon occurrence here – as Rossi's bike spent most of the race trying to flick him over the handlebars. Biaggi was the only man who could stay with Sete, but he had to back off after a big moment two laps from the flag. The Spaniard didn't get out of shape once, underlining his status as the best rain rider in MotoGP.

Barros started his season well with third place while still unfit from surgery over winter. Neil Hodgson rode brilliantly until a mechanical failure stopped his charge up the top ten.

2003 Gibernau crashed out of second place while chasing Rossi and effectively lost his chance of challenging for the championship. Biaggi was second and, in a good weekend for Ducati, Troy Bayliss finished third in his third GP after team-mate Capirossi set pole.

2002 Rossi ran away from them all on one of his favourite circuits, leaving Daijiro Kato on a two-stroke to duel with, and eventually beat, the other Honda V5 of Tohru Ukawa.

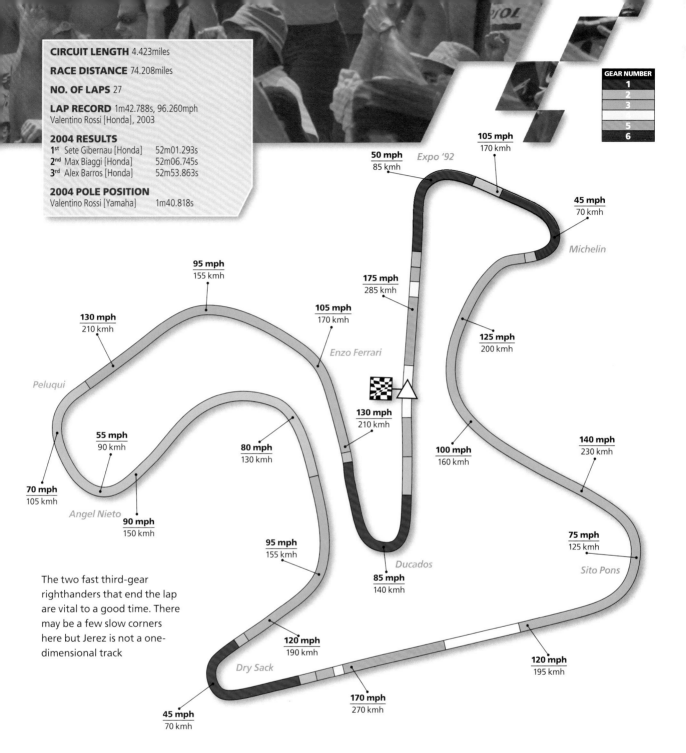

CIRCUIT LENGTH 4.423miles

RACE DISTANCE 74.208miles

NO. OF LAPS 27

LAP RECORD 1m42.788s, 96.260mph
Valentino Rossi [Honda], 2003

2004 RESULTS
1st Sete Gibernau [Honda]   52m01.293s
2nd Max Biaggi [Honda]   52m06.745s
3rd Alex Barros [Honda]   52m53.863s

2004 POLE POSITION
Valentino Rossi [Yamaha]   1m40.818s

GEAR NUMBER	
1	
2	
3	
5	
6	

105 mph / 170 kmh

50 mph / 85 kmh — Expo '92

45 mph / 70 kmh

Michelin

175 mph / 285 kmh

105 mph / 170 kmh — Enzo Ferrari

125 mph / 200 kmh

95 mph / 155 kmh

130 mph / 210 kmh — Peluqui

55 mph / 90 kmh

80 mph / 130 kmh

130 mph / 210 kmh

140 mph / 230 kmh

70 mph / 105 kmh

Angel Nieto

90 mph / 150 kmh

100 mph / 160 kmh

75 mph / 125 kmh — Sito Pons

95 mph / 155 kmh

85 mph / 140 kmh — Ducados

120 mph / 190 kmh

120 mph / 195 kmh

The two fast third-gear righthanders that end the lap are vital to a good time. There may be a few slow corners here but Jerez is not a one-dimensional track

Dry Sack

45 mph / 70 kmh

170 mph / 270 kmh

RIDER'S VIEW

"Every section of Jerez is important, though maybe the most important corners for a fast lap are the two last fast rights. There are a lot of long, fast turns which give the tyres a lot of g because you ride through them at very high lean angles, so you need good stability from the rear tyre casing, especially at the end of a race. Also, there is a lot of heavy braking so the front tyre needs to be able to handle some serious pressure, especially into Turn 1, into the hairpin at the end of the back straight and into the last turn."

Valentino Rossi

ROUND **2**

ESTORIL

17th April
ESTORIL
www.estoril-circuit.com

If ever there were a track of contrasts, it's Estoril: two ultra-fast corners, a kilometre-long straight plus the slowest section of the year. It's been a strangely low-key event in the past, but the late shuffling of the calendar gives it new-found prominence, so expect a bigger crowd than usual. Valentino Rossi has won every MotoGP race here, but as these wins came at the end of the European season his dominance hasn't seemed that important. (The only other senior winner here has been Garry McCoy in 2000.) The last thing the opposition needs this season is Rossi taking an easy 25 points in the second race of the year, forcing them to play catch-up so soon. Despite his success at the track, Valentino professes not to like the place very much!

The great imponderable at Estoril is always the weather. We've had wet-weather races, but the real problem is the wind. The track is high up above Estoril town and the resort of Cascais, with the Atlantic Ocean only four miles away, so gale-force winds are not uncommon. It's not unknown for 125s to be blown off the track, and even MotoGP bikes can be affected.

The track is on a plateau a good couple of hundred metres above sea level, and the ocean is only just out of the picture; it can get a little breezy

Autodromo Fernanda Pires da Silva

THE TRACK

Where is it?
Estoril is 20 miles west of Lisbon, the town merging with the seaside resort of Cascais to form one conurbation. The track is four miles inland towards Sintra.

Is it worth going to?
Why not? Lisbon is so close you can get in some serious tourism as well as race-watching. It won't take you much over half an hour to drive from central Lisbon to the track.

How do I get tickets?
There hasn't been a problem with paying on the gate in previous years, but you may want to check out www.estoril-circuit.com

Where do I watch from?
Two choices: the vast terraces on the outside of the start/finish straight give you a great view of pit lane and there is a giant screen. Alternatively, there are stands on the inside of the circuit, up between Curva 6 and the Esses, that give a good view of everything except the main straight.

Where does the overtaking happen?
Obviously, braking from top gear right down to first for Turn 1 is going to provide a favourite passing opportunity, but Barros prevented Gibernau from doing just that for most of last year's race. Curva 6 is generally reckoned the last passing place on the lap.

TV times
Same as UK time.

What should you eat and drink while watching the TV?
Carne de Porco Alentejana (stewed pork with clams) is the local speciality, with a bottle of Douro or Alentejo wine. Just a snack? Have a pastel de nata or two, it's like a custard cream in pastry, with a strong black coffee.

THE BIKES

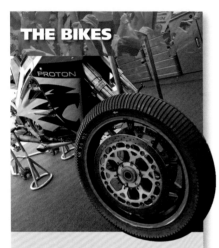

The two big problems are the contradictory requirements at different parts of the circuit and the changes in grip level as the track is cleaned. The wind doesn't just trouble riders in the corners, it also brings a lot of dust onto the little-used track. Because of the low grip levels, low to mid-range power must give the drive needed out of the half-dozen second-gear corners as well as the everlasting high-speed right-hander onto the main straight.

Chassis-wise, the first target is balanced, neutral geometry with good turn-in characteristics, but the bike must also cope with heavy braking. The base settings will be similar to those used at Donington, with slightly higher-rate fork springs to deal with the extra weight transfer under deceleration. The rear spring will be softer to improve feel under power although, as the circuit is quite narrow and there is limited grip off the racing line, the bike can't be allowed to run wide.

More attention is paid here than anywhere else to how the bike will behave at the end of the race, when the tyres are worn and grip is very low.

MotoGP @ ESTORIL

2004 Tamada took his first pole but Rossi toyed with him in the race and won, putting not just the Japanese rider but also Barros between himself and title rival Gibernau. (Sete has never had a rostrum finish here.) This was a major step for Rossi towards retaining the crown – and all the more impressive because he never expected to win.

Capirossi and the Ducati looked good through qualifying, but a first-lap coming-together with Biaggi put paid to that. Interestingly for the other Bridgestone-shod teams, John Hopkins had his highest-ever finishing position, in sixth.

2003 Another demolition job from Rossi, this time with Biaggi playing the mouse to Rossi's cat. Capirossi's Ducati started from pole and took third off Gibernau in the drag race out of the last corner.

2002 This one was wet, very wet, and should have been Gibernau's victory, yet Rossi still won. Pole-man Checa went backwards off the line with wheelspin in the first three gears but fought back to second in front of Ukawa. Sete was over 3.5 seconds in front when he crashed at the chicane, caught out by an erratic slipper clutch.

Valentino Rossi has won every MotoGP race ever held at Estoril; Sete Gibernau has yet to stand on the rostrum at the Portuguese track. The second race of the year should tell us a good deal about the season to come

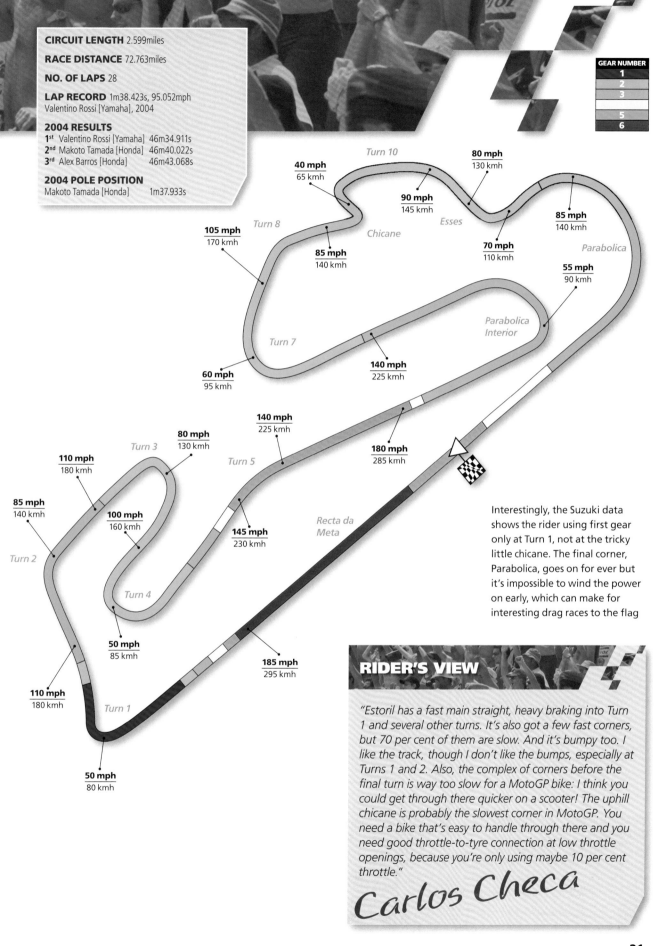

CIRCUIT LENGTH 2.599miles

RACE DISTANCE 72.763miles

NO. OF LAPS 28

LAP RECORD 1m38.423s, 95.052mph
Valentino Rossi [Yamaha], 2004

2004 RESULTS
1st Valentino Rossi [Yamaha] 46m34.911s
2nd Makoto Tamada [Honda] 46m40.022s
3rd Alex Barros [Honda] 46m43.068s

2004 POLE POSITION
Makoto Tamada [Honda] 1m37.933s

GEAR NUMBER
1
2
3
5
6

Turn 10

40 mph
65 Kmh

80 mph
130 kmh

90 mph
145 kmh

Esses

85 mph
140 kmh

Chicane

105 mph
170 kmh

85 mph
140 kmh

70 mph
110 kmh

Parabolica

55 mph
90 kmh

Turn 8

Turn 7

Parabolica Interior

60 mph
95 kmh

140 mph
225 kmh

140 mph
225 kmh

80 mph
130 kmh

Turn 3

Turn 5

110 mph
180 kmh

100 mph
160 kmh

180 mph
285 kmh

85 mph
140 kmh

Recta da Meta

145 mph
230 kmh

Turn 2

Turn 4

50 mph
85 kmh

185 mph
295 kmh

110 mph
180 kmh

Turn 1

50 mph
80 kmh

Interestingly, the Suzuki data
shows the rider using first gear
only at Turn 1, not at the tricky
little chicane. The final corner,
Parabolica, goes on for ever but
it's impossible to wind the power
on early, which can make for
interesting drag races to the flag

RIDER'S VIEW

*"Estoril has a fast main straight, heavy braking into Turn
1 and several other turns. It's also got a few fast corners,
but 70 per cent of them are slow. And it's bumpy too. I
like the track, though I don't like the bumps, especially at
Turns 1 and 2. Also, the complex of corners before the
final turn is way too slow for a MotoGP bike: I think you
could get through there quicker on a scooter! The uphill
chicane is probably the slowest corner in MotoGP. You
need a bike that's easy to handle through there and you
need good throttle-to-tyre connection at low throttle
openings, because you're only using maybe 10 per cent
throttle."*

Carlos Checa

ROUND **3**

SHANGHAI

1st May
SHANGHAI CIRCUIT
www.icsh.sh.cn

Shanghai Circuit

Even the ultra-rich of the Formula 1 paddock were gob-smacked at the scale of the circuit built to host international motorsport in the world's biggest market. Chinese authorities spent upwards of £250million on the track and its associated infrastructure and were rewarded with a successful debut car GP last year. The two aerofoil shaped wings over the start straight are the most obvious hallmark of the new design but that's not the end of it. Paddock offices are built on stilts over a lake, and the place is simply enormous. The track looks like an improved version of Sepang with the back straight over a kilometre long.

THE TRACK

Turn 1
Turn 2
Turn 5
Turn 3 & 4
Turn 7
Turn 6
Turn 8
Turn 9
Turn 14 & 15
Turn 16
Turn 11, 12 & 13
Turn 10

Where is it?
About 20 miles outside the city itself, north-east of Anting Town alongside Shanghai International Automobile City.

Is it worth going to?
Anyone with any travel lust in their soul has always wanted to go to China. Just remember you can't hire cars in China.

How do I get tickets?
Go to the website: it has a ticket booking link and helpful hints on local rules and regulations.

Where do I watch from?
The F1 race last year got 150,000 spectators, so anywhere you can buy a ticket for seems to be the answer.

Where will the overtaking happen?
Looks like there are plenty of places – even the cars managed to overtake.

TV times
Eight hours ahead of UK time.

What should you eat and drink while watching the TV?
As in the Chinese saying, anything with legs except a table.

RIDER'S VIEW

Roby Rolfo

"It looks like a car circuit just like Sepang, lots of corners that tighten up as they go on. That's fine if you have four wheels to brake with but difficult on a bike! However, there are also some long straights and fast corners which will be good on a MotoGP bike. That's important because there are too many circuits that are too slow. All in all I think it looks like a good compromise and it is so important that the Championship goes to China."

The architecture is stunning: even Schumacher the younger came out for a look at last year's F1 race

ROUND **4**

LE MANS

15th May
BUGATTI CIRCUIT LE MANS
www.gpfrancemoto.com

Le Mans

There can be few motorsport venues as famous as Le Mans. MotoGP uses the permanent short Bugatti Circuit, which only shares the section from the front straight round to La Chapelle (where the cars go straight on out into the country) with the 24-hour track. The rest of the circuit is quite twisty, but that first corner is the fastest bend of the year – how does flat out in sixth sound?

Le Mans itself is a medium-sized industrial city with a small but charming and historic old town. It is easy to get to by road from Paris or the Channel ports, and the TGV high-speed train only takes an hour-and-a-half from Paris. Accommodation in the city itself is usually full up with team personnel, so if you haven't the stamina for the three massive but, um, lively campsites you'll be in one of the neighbouring towns like Alençon. If you camp, the local authorities are very keen to keep you at the circuit so there is always a good programme of bands and other entertainment to keep you amused.

Carlos Checa has always gone well at Le Mans; he was on the front row and the rostrum last year having led the first half of the race

THE TRACK

Where is it?
About 125 miles south-west of Paris and almost exactly the same distance directly south of Caen and the Normandy coast. The track is south of the city, just outside the ring road.

Is it worth going to?
Le Mans is the nearest GP to the UK and is therefore easy to get to. You probably know a bit of the language, so get over there!

How do I get tickets?
Pay at the gate, but preferably during qualifying, not on race day. Check out www.gpfrancemoto.com

Where do I watch from?
One of the good things about Le Mans is that your entry ticket gets you everywhere. The grandstand outside that awesome first turn is a fabulous place to watch from and the chicane just over the hill guarantees plenty of close-up action – but claim your spot early on Sunday.

Where does the overtaking happen?
Le Mans has lots of hard braking spots and therefore plenty of outbraking opportunities. For heart-in-mouth stuff, look out for slipstreaming down the straight followed by line-stealing through that first corner, with the move being completed on the brakes for the chicane.

TV times
One hour ahead of UK time.

What should you eat and drink while watching the TV?
What else but steak frites and a nice bottle of red? Follow it with a tarte tatin – and may I recommend a calvados (apple brandy) afterwards?

MotoGP @ LE MANS

2004 Spain ruled, with Gibernau and Checa first and second both on the grid and in the race. Biaggi and Rossi fought for third, with Max coming out ahead. Sete had won the previous race at Jerez: this was the first time he'd had two victories in a row and the first time he'd been at the top of the points table. Most of the talk, though, was about an incident before the start, when Rossi stalled on the grid and appeared to receive illegal assistance to restart.

2003 The first of only two occasions when wet-weather rules were applied. After a red flag, the field reassembled to decide the race over just the remaining 13 laps. On a patchy track Rossi rode the dry parts best – but Gibernau rode the wet parts better, and won. Barros was third on a Yamaha. Nobody complained about the regulations.

2002 It rained again and under the old rules the race was declared over when the red flags went out after 21 of 28 laps. Rossi had understood the situation and moved to the front just a couple of laps earlier. He won from team-mate Ukawa and Biaggi.

THE BIKES

The circuit is made up of second-gear hairpins linked by straights, with only the occasional chicane breaking up the pattern. It doesn't cause the teams too many set-up problems. Stability on the brakes is the main requirement, even at the expense of agility on corner turn-in, as the stopwatch shows that the gains on braking far outweigh what can be made up on corner entry.

As at Jerez, a firm front end is necessary to deal with the sudden weight transfer as the rider gets off the brakes and onto the throttle – and vice versa. Spring rates will therefore be the highest used anywhere to deal with the braking forces and damping will also be stiff to control pitching. Low rear ride height helps keep the rear tyre on the deck; this reduces the ability to hold a line while exiting a corner, so a soft rear spring rate will be used for feel, but with lots of preload to prevent the rear from squatting under power. A less linear rear linkage will also feature to cope with the on/off nature of the way the power is used. Le Mans is not a problem for tyres as most of the corners are very short.

Last year's win put Sete Gibernau to the top of the points table for the first time in his career

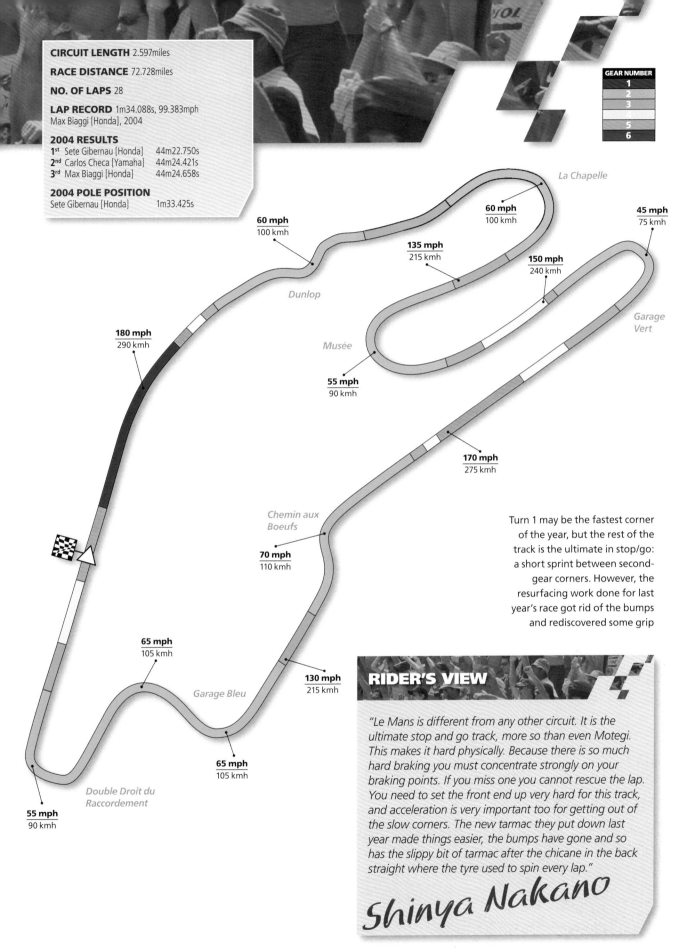

CIRCUIT LENGTH 2.597miles

RACE DISTANCE 72.728miles

NO. OF LAPS 28

LAP RECORD 1m34.088s, 99.383mph
Max Biaggi [Honda], 2004

2004 RESULTS
1st Sete Gibernau [Honda]   44m22.750s
2nd Carlos Checa [Yamaha]   44m24.421s
3rd Max Biaggi [Honda]   44m24.658s

2004 POLE POSITION
Sete Gibernau [Honda]   1m33.425s

GEAR NUMBER
1
2
3
4
5
6

La Chapelle

60 mph / 100 kmh

45 mph / 75 kmh

60 mph / 100 kmh

Dunlop

135 mph / 215 kmh

150 mph / 240 kmh

Garage Vert

Musée

55 mph / 90 kmh

180 mph / 290 kmh

170 mph / 275 kmh

Chemin aux Boeufs

70 mph / 110 kmh

Turn 1 may be the fastest corner of the year, but the rest of the track is the ultimate in stop/go: a short sprint between second-gear corners. However, the resurfacing work done for last year's race got rid of the bumps and rediscovered some grip

130 mph / 215 kmh

Garage Bleu

65 mph / 105 kmh

65 mph / 105 kmh

Double Droit du Raccordement

55 mph / 90 kmh

RIDER'S VIEW

"Le Mans is different from any other circuit. It is the ultimate stop and go track, more so than even Motegi. This makes it hard physically. Because there is so much hard braking you must concentrate strongly on your braking points. If you miss one you cannot rescue the lap. You need to set the front end up very hard for this track, and acceleration is very important too for getting out of the slow corners. The new tarmac they put down last year made things easier, the bumps have gone and so has the slippy bit of tarmac after the chicane in the back straight where the tyre used to spin every lap."

Shinya Nakano

ROUND 5
MUGELLO

5th June
AUTODROMO INTERNAZIONALE DEL MUGELLO
www.mugellocircuit.it

Only in Italy would you find such a magnificent track set in such beautiful scenery. Mugello is in an area of Tuscany just north of Florence, so you just know everything will be perfect: countryside, food, general laid-back attitude to life. Now pack in tens of thousands of rabid Italian fans lining either side of the valley that the track runs up and down and you have motorsport heaven. All this plus the fastest top speed of the year – and just to make it really interesting the bikes crest a rise on the straight just before they start braking for a second-gear corner. Only Phillip Island comes close in the competition for most awesome stretch of GP tarmac. At some places you might make the mistake of thinking that you could ride with the guys out there. At Mugello the thought would never enter your head.

The only problems are getting in and out of the place and finding a room. There is no town of any size between the track and Florence, so if you don't fancy camping at the circuit you'll have a long day on Sunday. The main entrance is down a single-track road so you can be stuck inside the circuit for many hours after the race.

Will Ducati reclaim the top speed crown on their home ground? Will anyone challenge the Italians on their home ground? What colour will Marco Melandri dye his hair?

Autodromo Internazionale del Mugello

THE TRACK

Where is it?
Just under 20 miles north-north-east of Florence, near the town of Borgo San Lorenzo. Use the A1 autostrada from Florence to Bologna (which is about 40 miles further on) and take the Barberino di Mugello exit.

Is it worth going to?
Oh God, yes: Mugello is one of the tracks that you must visit once during your spectating career. Florence airport is a short drive away, Bologna only a little further. Pick the right spot to watch from and your racing brain will be recalibrated. There's also the small matter of MotoGP's top speed record, set on this straight.

How do I get tickets?
Buy beforehand from www.mugellocircuit.it or from the ticket office in the village of Scarperia that adjoins the circuit. You can pay on the gate but race day is complete mayhem so get organised early.

Where do I watch from?
As the main straight is in the bottom of a valley and the track runs up the slopes either side you are hard put to find a bad place to watch from. The Italian riders' fan clubs stake out their own areas and the Ducati factory packs the Correntaio grandstand.

Where does the overtaking happen?
Judging by last year, everywhere!

TV times
One hour ahead of UK time.

What should you eat and drink while watching the TV?
Pizza and a Nastro Azzuro if you're in a hurry; pasta followed by pan-fried chicken escalope with lemon and rosemary washed down with a nice Chianti if you're not.

THE BIKES

Mugello is a circuit that requires the best from every aspect of a racing motorcycle. The aim is to find balanced geometry that lets the rider change direction quickly through this high-speed roller-coaster, especially the tricky right-hander at the end of the main straight. This corner is the key to a fast time as it dramatically affects the next sequence of turns. For the same reason, the front end will need to give good feedback under braking into the numerous downhill turns, especially the one onto the front straight. This involves lowering the front, which also lightens the handling through the high-speed Esses that make up a lot of the track. Linear medium-damping characteristics will be dialled in, a must to aid feel as there are no bumps on the way into the corners.

There are some bumps on corner exits, so to find the necessary drive a medium-to- high rear spring rate will be used, along with a progressive rear linkage to prevent squat as riders wind the power on out of the positively cambered corners.

MotoGP @ MUGELLO

2004 What didn't happen? After the rain came and the red flags went out the race was decided over the six laps that remained. They restarted on a damp track – with that 200mph straight in front of them! After countless lead changes Rossi won the shortest-ever GP. The 17 laps that counted for nothing before the red flag saw over 35 changes of lead and the fastest crash anyone can remember. Nakano's rear tyre blew and sent him tumbling down the track. Remarkably, he suffered no serious injury. Fellow Bridgestone runner Tamada pulled out when his tyre chunked after he'd diced with the leaders. This six-lap dash caused a rethink of the wet-weather regulations, but it was noticeable that the three guys who were leading when the race was stopped were also the ones standing on the rostrum.

2003 Rossi won, surviving a late charge from Capirossi, with Biaggi third for an all-Italian rostrum. Makoto Tamada announced himself with a ride through the field from tenth on the grid to fourth at the flag. Ducati set a new top-speed mark in qualifying.

Mugello's race is everything a GP should be; fast, fabulous and just a little crazy

2002 Rossi won from Biaggi with Ukawa third, and was then booked for speeding and a variety of offences by two traffic cops: his fan club's merry post-race jape. Ukawa set a new best maximum speed record and there was a mass track invasion on the slow-down lap.

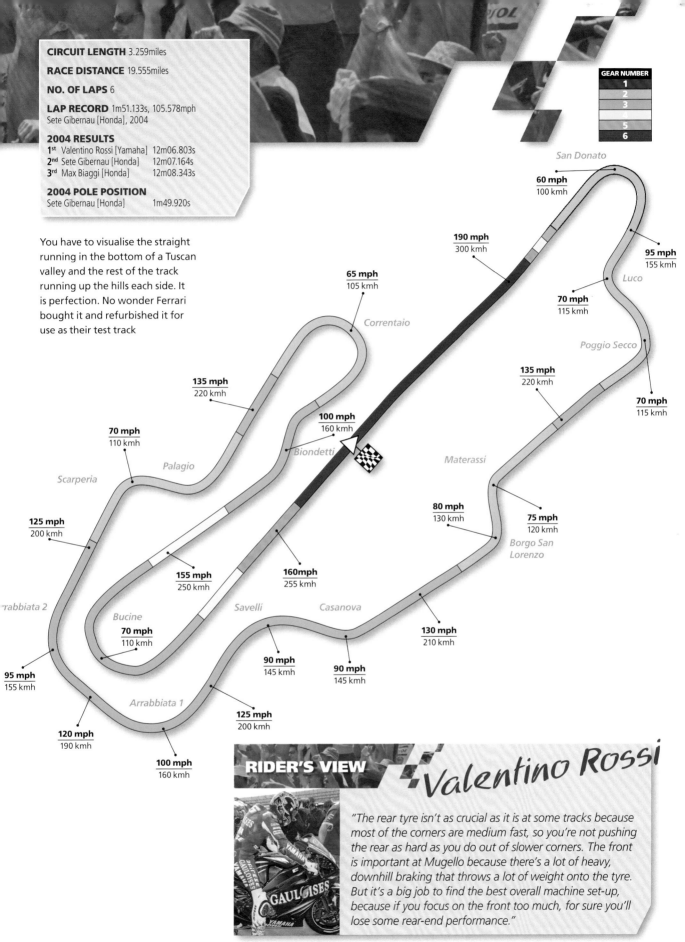

CIRCUIT LENGTH 3.259miles

RACE DISTANCE 19.555miles

NO. OF LAPS 6

LAP RECORD 1m51.133s, 105.578mph
Sete Gibernau [Honda], 2004

2004 RESULTS
1st Valentino Rossi [Yamaha] 12m06.803s
2nd Sete Gibernau [Honda] 12m07.164s
3rd Max Biaggi [Honda] 12m08.343s

2004 POLE POSITION
Sete Gibernau [Honda] 1m49.920s

GEAR NUMBER

| 1 |
| 2 |
| 3 |
| 4 |
| 5 |
| 6 |

You have to visualise the straight running in the bottom of a Tuscan valley and the rest of the track running up the hills each side. It is perfection. No wonder Ferrari bought it and refurbished it for use as their test track

San Donato

60 mph
100 kmh

95 mph
155 kmh

Luco

190 mph
300 kmh

70 mph
115 kmh

Poggio Secco

65 mph
105 kmh

Correntaio

135 mph
220 kmh

70 mph
115 kmh

135 mph
220 kmh

70 mph
110 kmh

Palagio

100 mph
160 kmh

Biondetti

Materassi

Scarperia

80 mph
130 kmh

75 mph
120 kmh

125 mph
200 kmh

Borgo San Lorenzo

155 mph
250 kmh

160mph
255 kmh

Savelli

Casanova

130 mph
210 kmh

Arrabbiata 2

Bucine

70 mph
110 kmh

90 mph
145 kmh

90 mph
145 kmh

95 mph
155 kmh

Arrabbiata 1

125 mph
200 kmh

120 mph
190 kmh

100 mph
160 kmh

RIDER'S VIEW *Valentino Rossi*

"The rear tyre isn't as crucial as it is at some tracks because most of the corners are medium fast, so you're not pushing the rear as hard as you do out of slower corners. The front is important at Mugello because there's a lot of heavy, downhill braking that throws a lot of weight onto the tyre. But it's a big job to find the best overall machine set-up, because if you focus on the front too much, for sure you'll lose some rear-end performance."

31

ROUND **6**

CATALUNYA

12th June
CIRCUIT DE CATALUNYA
www.circuitcat.com

The majority of the Spanish racers, including Gibernau, Checa, Xaus, Elias and Pedrosa, are Catalans hailing from the Barcelona area. Dorna – the company that runs GPs – has its offices in Barcelona. This is a race that matters. It also helps that the fabulous city of

Barcelona is just up the road. So if you want to understand how important the sport of motorcycle racing is in Spain (and spend some time in one of Europe's more interesting cities), this is the race to see.

The circuit has a lot going for it,

including total resurfacing over winter. It is a great test of machinery – what works here tends to work anywhere – so pay attention to qualifying as well as the race to get some pointers for the rest of the year. Oddly, the locals don't tend to turn up in any numbers during qualifying but they fill the place to overflowing on race day, creating a sizzling atmosphere that borders on mass hysteria if one of the aforementioned local heroes looks like winning. Expect some of the lesser-known local boys in the 250 and 125cc classes to punch above their weight in response to all that support as well.

The noise of a gridful of MotoGP bikes echoes wonderfully off the giant grandstand opposite the pits complex

Circuit de Catalunya

THE TRACK

Where is it?
The Circuit de Catalunya isn't in Barcelona, it's just outside Granollers, on an industrial estate less than an hour's drive from the city centre. If you're driving to and from the airport be aware that the motorways can do good impersonations of the M25.

Is it worth going to?
If you want to see how good a modern circuit can be then this is the place to go. No stupid chicanes, a 200mph straight, good viewing facilities and civilised amenities. And Barcelona is only just up the road.

How do I get tickets?
Go to www.circuitcat.com if you want a grandstand seat. You can always pay on the day but you'll be standing to watch the races.

Where do I watch from?
The giant grandstand on the straight gives a good view of much of the last part of the circuit, but the great arc of terracing at the highest section of the track overlooks most of the action zones. Go to Turn 4 for the best sideways thrills of the year.

Where does the overtaking happen?
Get out of the last corner well, slipstream the bloke in front down the 200mph straight and outbrake him at Turn 1 – that's the favourite option, but there are plenty of others. Even the last corner has been known to work.

TV times
One hour ahead of UK time.

What should you eat and drink while watching the TV?
It's sausage again! This time the spicy Catalan variety. You should eat it with bread which you have first rubbed with a ripe tomato. Drink wine.

THE BIKES

Front-end feel in the long sweeping bends is a key concern, but it must be found without sacrificing the overall balance of the machine because of the amount of time spent on part-throttle on the sides of the tyres before punching out onto the next straight. As at Mugello, there will be only small changes from base set-up, this time looking for a little extra front-end bias. Most of this will be achieved by suspension adjustment, however, not through chassis modifications.

Suspension doesn't like working when the bike is on full lean, so slightly softer springs will be used to help cope with any of the bumps on the corners which haven't been removed during resurfacing while the preload will be wound up to compensate for any resulting g-forces. Damping will be slightly softer on compression and rebound, but rear spring preload will be very similar to Mugello, to stop the bike from squatting and then running wide under power. This is especially important in the long, right-handed run onto the front straight, which determines the ultimate top speed and slipstream potential.

Tyres have a hard time and grip levels can change from session to session, which makes picking something that'll last the race difficult. Engines need all the mid- and top-end power they can get.

Rossi's 2004 win in Gibernau's back yard was the start of the realisation that he really could win the championship on a Yamaha

MotoGP @ CATALUNYA

2004 Rossi wasn't supposed to win here but he did, after seeing off a spirited challenge from Gibernau. Marco Melandri took third place and his first MotoGP rostrum. Ducati had a terrible time at the track where they'd won in 2003 and both Repsol Hondas failed to finish: Hayden suffered a holed radiator and Barros crashed while looking good early on. Nakano took seventh off Biaggi on the last corner just one week after his terrifying 200mph Mugello crash.

2003 History was made when Capirossi took Ducati's first victory in MotoGP. Rossi ran off the track when he nearly tailgated the Ducati, then charged back from sixth place and a five-second deficit to be three seconds down on Loris at the flag. It took him just one lap and one corner to pass Nakano, Checa, Biaggi (twice) and Gibernau, but Capirossi was just far enough away to take the win.

2002 Local hero Carlos Checa gave the Repsol Hondas of Rossi and Ukawa a hard time but he faded to third in the last part of the race. The team-mates fought to the flag, with Rossi winning by under a second.

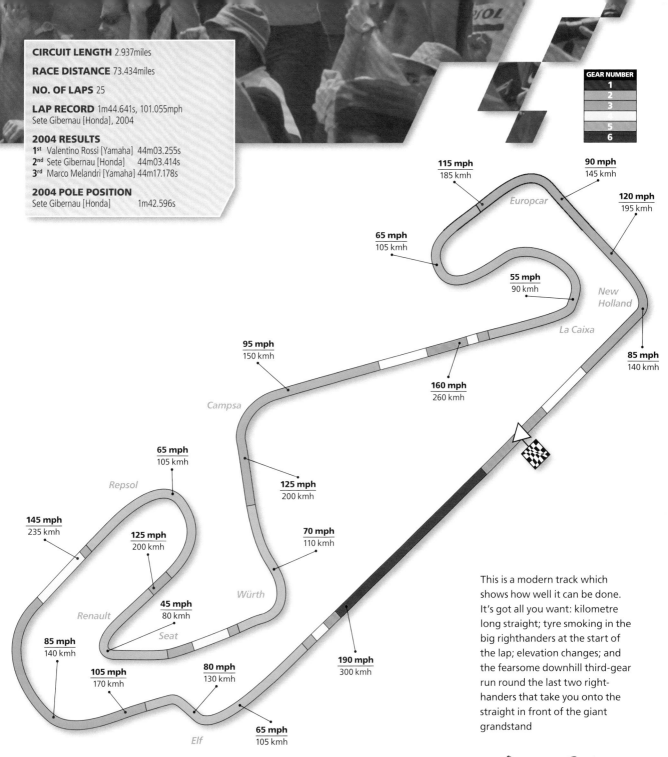

CIRCUIT LENGTH 2.937miles

RACE DISTANCE 73.434miles

NO. OF LAPS 25

LAP RECORD 1m44.641s, 101.055mph
Sete Gibernau [Honda], 2004

2004 RESULTS
1st Valentino Rossi [Yamaha] 44m03.255s
2nd Sete Gibernau [Honda] 44m03.414s
3rd Marco Melandri [Yamaha] 44m17.178s

2004 POLE POSITION
Sete Gibernau [Honda] 1m42.596s

GEAR NUMBER	
	1
	2
	3
	4
	5
	6

115 mph / 185 kmh

90 mph / 145 kmh

120 mph / 195 kmh

Europcar

65 mph / 105 kmh

55 mph / 90 kmh

New Holland

La Caixa

85 mph / 140 kmh

95 mph / 150 kmh

160 mph / 260 kmh

Campsa

65 mph / 105 kmh

125 mph / 200 kmh

Repsol

145 mph / 235 kmh

125 mph / 200 kmh

70 mph / 110 kmh

Würth

45 mph / 80 kmh

Renault

Seat

85 mph / 140 kmh

105 mph / 170 kmh

80 mph / 130 kmh

190 mph / 300 kmh

65 mph / 105 kmh

Elf

This is a modern track which shows how well it can be done. It's got all you want: kilometre long straight; tyre smoking in the big righthanders at the start of the lap; elevation changes; and the fearsome downhill third-gear run round the last two right-handers that take you onto the straight in front of the giant grandstand

RIDER'S VIEW

Carlos Checa

"The grip situation is always strange. On days when there's no grip, you come into the pits and you can wipe the dust off your wheel rims. On grippy days, there's no dust on the wheels. I think wind blows dust onto the track, maybe from the gravel traps which are full of volcanic stone. The front tyre is more important here than at most circuits. You need stability and grip, especially for the downhill corner entries (like Turns 1 and 5), some of which are quite bumpy. You need the tyre and suspension working together, offering both flexibility and stability, so they can 'copy' the bumps."

ROUND **7**

ASSEN

25th June

CIRCUIT VAN DRENTHE
www.tt-assen.com

Circuit van Drenthe

Assen is the only track that has hosted a GP every year since the inception of the World Championships in 1949, and you can feel the tradition in every aspect of the Circuit van Drenthe. No computer would have produced such a trace of tarmac: the track is all corners but still manages to have the fastest lap record speed of the year, and it hasn't been significantly altered by recent modifications. This is a circuit the riders, almost without exception, love to race on despite its unique mix of interconnected and adverse camber turns – thanks to the crown in the middle it's just like the roads you ride on.

Spectators come from all over Europe to pack the huge grandstand and grass banks that line the circuit. The authorities have stopped fans building their own mini-stands, but old hands still bring acres of plastic sheeting for protection from the inevitable showers. They've also cracked down on bringing alcohol into the track, but Assen town remains party central on Friday night thanks to Dutch tolerance and good humour. Traditionally, this is the first overseas GP that British fans go to, and once you've been you'll definitely want to go back.

Assen is a track like no other: the cathedral of bike racing, Europe's meeting place, and a stupendously enjoyable place to watch a motorcycle race

THE TRACK

Where is it?
Assen is just over 100 miles north of Amsterdam and 15 miles south of Groningen. The local airport is used by one or two budget airlines, otherwise fly to Amsterdam and drive, or take a ferry to Hook of Holland.

Is it worth going to?
The circuit is due to be drastically shortened over winter, so go and see the full majesty of the longest and fastest track on the calendar while you still can.

How do I get tickets?
You can still pay on the day and find a place on the grass banks, but get there early if you want a decent spot. Grandstand tickets tend to sell out straight after the previous race. Check out www.tt-assen.com

Where do I watch from?
Any seat will have a good view. At some point in the weekend get down to the Veenslang and gape at the top-gear kerb-to-kerb run. The new overhanging grandstand at the chicane looks like it'll be a great place to watch from.

Where does the overtaking happen?
Turn 1, the chicane, on the inside at de Strubben, Stekkenwal – almost anywhere. There are some places where bikes can't pass but, like the high-speed run to the last corner, they're building up to a pass.

TV times
One hour ahead of UK time.

What should you eat and drink while watching the TV?
Chips with a dollop of mayonnaise and copious quantities of lager.

THE BIKES

Assen is one of those tracks you must see at some point in your career as a MotoGP fan, and fortunately it's easy to get to!

A chassis is needed that's both agile and stable – mutually exclusive requirements. There won't be many deviations from the base setting; suspension tuning and tyre profile will be the variable factors. The rear spring will be stiffened because of the g-forces generated in high-speed corners, but the compression damping will be softer for feel. At the front, the springs will be softened because of the lack of really hard braking areas. Teams will always have an eye on the weather and be thinking about a set-up for the rain. It may be a cliché to say that Assen is a riders' circuit but it's true: the crews can only do so much, then it's down to the rider to work with the bike he's got.

MotoGP @ ASSEN

2004 A last-lap move that Rossi put on Gibernau saw the Spaniard almost tailgate his rival: Sete finished the race with a broken front mudguard and in a very dark frame of mind. For the third GP running – Mugello, Catalunya, the Netherlands – Rossi and Yamaha had won at a track that was supposed to favour the Hondas. It was a crucial moment in the fight for the title, when Rossi truly started to believe he could retain his crown.

2003 The race was so wet and dismal the bikes should have used headlamps. Gibernau proved his mastery of the wet with a runaway, make that splashaway, win. Biaggi took second, beating Rossi (who finished third) for the first time on the same machinery. Wild-card Hofmann soundly trounced the other Kawasaki riders to guarantee a full-time ride in 2004.

2002 Alex Barros used the agility of his 500cc two-stroke to harass the relatively unwieldy four-strokes down the Veenslang, at one point taking two at a time. But Rossi always had top speed in hand and blasted past on the front straight to win. Checa took third despite Ukawa crashing into him at the final corner.

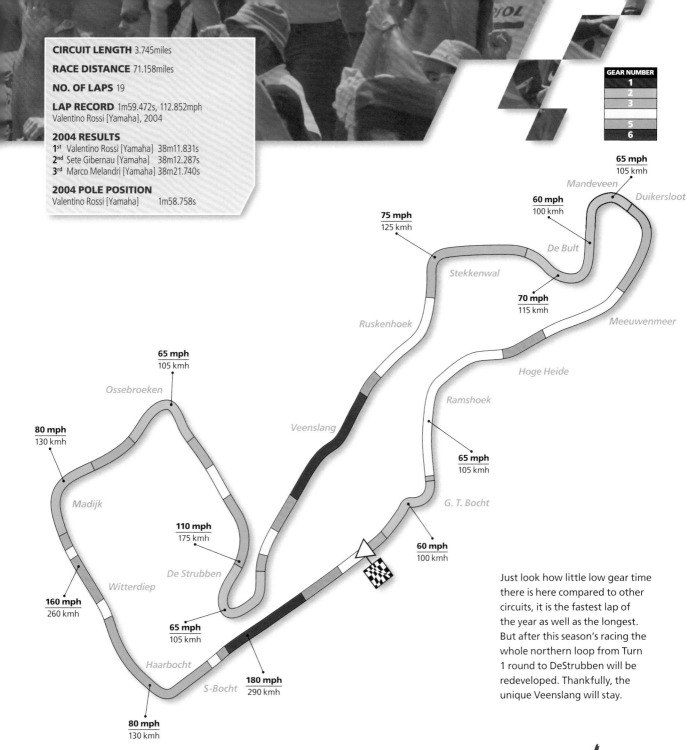

CIRCUIT LENGTH 3.745miles

RACE DISTANCE 71.158miles

NO. OF LAPS 19

LAP RECORD 1m59.472s, 112.852mph
Valentino Rossi [Yamaha], 2004

2004 RESULTS
1st Valentino Rossi [Yamaha] 38m11.831s
2nd Sete Gibernau [Yamaha] 38m12.287s
3rd Marco Melandri [Yamaha] 38m21.740s

2004 POLE POSITION
Valentino Rossi [Yamaha] 1m58.758s

GEAR NUMBER
1
2
3
5
6

65 mph
105 kmh
Mandeveen

Duikersloot

60 mph
100 kmh

De Bult

75 mph
125 kmh

Stekkenwal

70 mph
115 kmh

Meeuwenmeer

Ruskenhoek

Hoge Heide

65 mph
105 kmh
Ossebroeken

Ramshoek

80 mph
130 kmh

Madijk

Veenslang

65 mph
105 kmh

G. T. Bocht

110 mph
175 kmh

60 mph
100 kmh

160 mph
260 kmh

Witterdiep

De Strubben

65 mph
105 kmh

Haarbocht

180 mph
290 kmh

S-Bocht

80 mph
130 kmh

Just look how little low gear time there is here compared to other circuits, it is the fastest lap of the year as well as the longest. But after this season's racing the whole northern loop from Turn 1 round to DeStrubben will be redeveloped. Thankfully, the unique Veenslang will stay.

RIDER'S VIEW

Colin Edwards

"Man, it's so fast, every time you go there you've got to adjust your eyes because everything's going by so quick. It's one of those places where every single corner is important – you have to link it all – every corner leads to the next which leads to the next. But Assen can be an evil place when it wants to be. The camber can bite you. It makes you feel so comfortable, so nice, then you get to mid-corner and the track rises and drops away from you, so if you're not careful it's 'Sayonara!', you're out of there! The grip level is just unbelievable, especially in the wet – you can throw the bike on your knee on our Michelin rain tyres."

ROUND **8**
LAGUNA SECA

10th July
LAGUNA SECA RACEWAY
www.laguna-seca.com

There aren't many better places to be than this part of California. Monterey, where Steinbeck wrote Cannery Row, is just up the road on the coast. Carmel, where Clint Eastwood was mayor, is just to the south on the way to the Hearst Castle and the beauty of Big Sur. Highway 1 hugs the coast of the Pacific Ocean, where you can go whale watching, and see fur seals and sea otters. Basically, it's paradise.

Everybody knows about the Corkscrew, but it's the run up to the highest part of the track and the high-speed kink in the front straight that is Turn 2 you need to keep an eye on during racing

RIDER'S VIEW — *John Hopkins*

"It's going to be quite interesting going through Turn 1 – it doesn't look like a corner on TV but we're going to have both wheels drifting through there. That should make the braking for Turn 2 kinda fun. The Corkscrew is really just another corner but the run to the Corkscrew out of Turn 7 is going to be real interesting. Back in 2001 when I was riding Formula Extreme there I used to have both tyres just skimming the ground over the crest, but those bikes were much heavier than a MotoGP machine. I'm positive we're going to have both wheels right off the ground there. That could make the braking for the Corkscrew kinda interesting too."

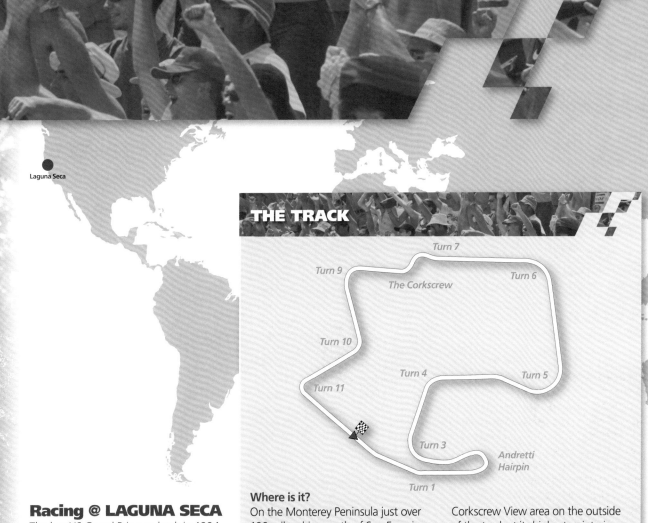

Laguna Seca

THE TRACK

Turn 7
Turn 9
Turn 6
The Corkscrew
Turn 10
Turn 4
Turn 5
Turn 11
Turn 3
Andretti
Hairpin
Turn 1

Racing @ LAGUNA SECA

The last US Grand Prix was back in 1994 when Luca Cadalora won on a Yamaha from John Kocinski (Cagiva) and Mick Doohan (Honda). The American Cagiva rider had the satisfaction of setting the fastest lap at 1min 26.444sec. From '95 until last year, the only date in Laguna's calendar for international bike racing was occupied by the Superbikes. That lap record belongs to Noriyuki Haga at 1min 25.475sec and was set in 2002. Last year Chris Vermeulen did 1min 26.798sec on control tyres.

Don't expect to see any 125s or 250s this weekend; the MotoGP grid is sharing the paddock with the domestic AMA Championship field. The Superbike race featuring Neil Hodgson (Ducati) against multiple champ Mat Mladin (Suzuki) will make interesting viewing, as will Saturday's kart race. Karts? SuperKarts actually, with ex-two wheel champs Wayne Rainey, Eddie Lawson and Kevin Schwantz among the drivers.

Seeing Wayne racing again promises to be an emotional experience for many in the paddock.

Where is it?
On the Monterey Peninsula just over 100 miles drive south of San Francisco.

Is it worth going to?
Are you joking? It's always worth going to California, and especially this bit of it. The track has a splendid variety of corners and major elevation changes, plus one of the most famous corners in world racing.

On the tourism front you can do culture in Monterey, or gawp at the scenery down Highway 1. Then there are the wineries, San Francisco, the valleys; you could even keep on driving down to LA.

How do I get tickets?
www.laguna-seca.com has all the info you need. Don't fly without a ticket, they tend to get big crowds at America's only world championship road racing event of the year.

Where do I watch from?
The grandstands are small and will obviously be full but the new

Corkscrew View area on the outside of the track at its highest point gives a great vista over the last part of the lap. The hillside on the outside of Turn 2 has similar advantages.

Where does the overtaking happen?
Wayne Rainey always reckoned that passing someone in the blind braking area before the Corkscrew stopped them bothering you again. More conventionally, the final turn is a classic outbraking site. The double-apex Turn 2 makes for spectacular passes on the exit; get it right on the entry and the other guy will look like he's standing still as you head for Turn 3.

TV times
Eight hours behind UK time.

What should you eat and drink while watching the TV?
Burgers and a weak beer in the cheap seats; seafood and a chilled zinfandel in corporate hospitality.

ROUND **9**
DONINGTON

24th July
DONINGTON PARK
www.donington-park.co.uk

Last year the track was completely resurfaced, next year the pits complex gets a major facelift, but in the meantime we'll have to make do with what we have. Hopefully the appalling traffic problems of last year – when some fans couldn't get out of the car park for six hours – won't be repeated. Leaving the basic facilities to one side though, there is still nothing to compare with the sight of the field streaming down the Craner Curves, one of the most awe-inspiring stretches of tarmac on the entire calendar. In fact from the start right round to Foggy's, the track is fabulous, but then come the two hairpins, making three first-gear corners in a row. Eddie Lawson famously called it 'the car-park section'. Donington really is a game of two halves.

Donington's best feature is the museum, situated by the main entrance at Coppice Corner. It houses a quite astonishing collection of Formula 1 cars and automobilia put together by Tom Wheatcroft, the man who restored the circuit in the 1970s. And now that the track has a long-term contract to host the race, the leaseholders can justify upgrading the facilities.

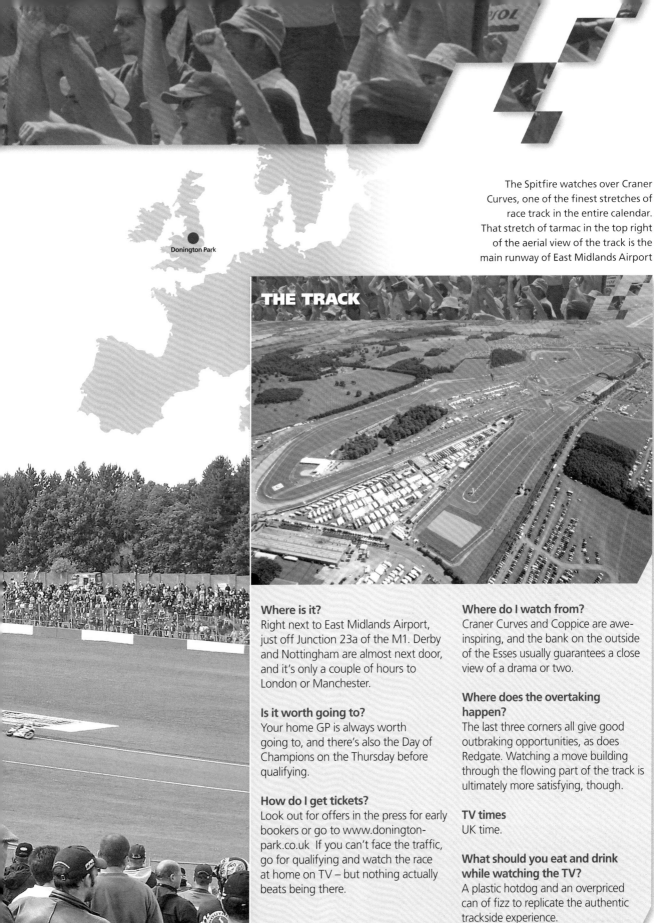

The Spitfire watches over Craner Curves, one of the finest stretches of race track in the entire calendar. That stretch of tarmac in the top right of the aerial view of the track is the main runway of East Midlands Airport

Donington Park

THE TRACK

Where is it?
Right next to East Midlands Airport, just off Junction 23a of the M1. Derby and Nottingham are almost next door, and it's only a couple of hours to London or Manchester.

Is it worth going to?
Your home GP is always worth going to, and there's also the Day of Champions on the Thursday before qualifying.

How do I get tickets?
Look out for offers in the press for early bookers or go to www.donington-park.co.uk If you can't face the traffic, go for qualifying and watch the race at home on TV – but nothing actually beats being there.

Where do I watch from?
Craner Curves and Coppice are awe-inspiring, and the bank on the outside of the Esses usually guarantees a close view of a drama or two.

Where does the overtaking happen?
The last three corners all give good outbraking opportunities, as does Redgate. Watching a move building through the flowing part of the track is ultimately more satisfying, though.

TV times
UK time.

What should you eat and drink while watching the TV?
A plastic hotdog and an overpriced can of fizz to replicate the authentic trackside experience.

THE BIKES

The main aim is to find a chassis that offers a good pitching balance during braking and acceleration. Too much and stability under brakes is lost in the second half of the lap; not enough and the bike will be difficult to manoeuvre through the fast, sweeping turns that make up the first part of the lap. The catch is that the first half of the circuit lends itself to a fast lap time, while a good set-up for the second half – from Fogarty's to Goddard's – is where an easy pass can be made if the bike allows it.

The undulating first part of the circuit also pushes the front of the bike a lot, while the second half is pretty much 'highside' territory. Softer spring rates front and rear, with the fine-tuning left to the spring preload, will be the way to go. This approach will help drive and improve feedback from the front, although the trade-off will be a loss of stability on the brakes into the hairpins.

As for the motor, lots of midrange is what's required: this isn't an outright speed or power circuit.

MotoGP @ DONINGTON

2004 Rossi won from the Telefonica Hondas, with Colin Edwards taking his first MotoGP rostrum in front of team-mate Gibernau. The crucial moment was when Rossi kept pressing just as a flurry of rain came across the circuit, while the others knocked the throttle off by a fraction. Biaggi had a shocker and ended up twelfth; Troy Bayliss broke the world damp grass-tracking record at Craner after a near-highsider but still finished fifth.

2003 Rossi thought he'd won after Biaggi went straight on at the Esses, but hours later Race Direction decided he had passed Capirossi under a yellow flag on lap 2. He was docked six seconds and relegated to third behind Max and Gibernau. This incident led to revisions of the punishments for yellow-flag offences.

2002 Ukawa destroyed a V5 at the bottom of Craner in qualifying. Rossi also fell and banged his head. In the race, Checa led until half-distance when pressure from Rossi and the bumps at Goddard's undid him. Biaggi and Barros followed the Doctor home.

The Doctor has taken the chequered flag first in all three MotoGP races at Donington but won only two of them

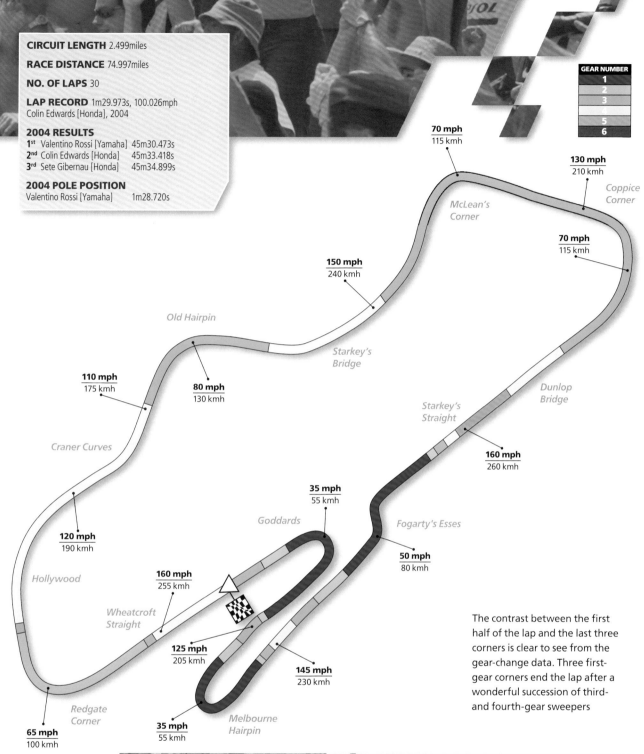

CIRCUIT LENGTH 2.499miles

RACE DISTANCE 74.997miles

NO. OF LAPS 30

LAP RECORD 1m29.973s, 100.026mph
Colin Edwards [Honda], 2004

2004 RESULTS
1st Valentino Rossi [Yamaha] 45m30.473s
2nd Colin Edwards [Honda] 45m33.418s
3rd Sete Gibernau [Honda] 45m34.899s

2004 POLE POSITION
Valentino Rossi [Yamaha] 1m28.720s

GEAR NUMBER	
1	
2	
3	
4	
5	
6	

70 mph
115 kmh

130 mph
210 kmh

Coppice Corner

McLean's Corner

70 mph
115 kmh

150 mph
240 kmh

Old Hairpin

Starkey's Bridge

Dunlop Bridge

110 mph
175 kmh

80 mph
130 kmh

Starkey's Straight

160 mph
260 kmh

Craner Curves

35 mph
55 kmh

Goddards

Fogarty's Esses

120 mph
190 kmh

50 mph
80 kmh

Hollywood

160 mph
255 kmh

Wheatcroft Straight

125 mph
205 kmh

145 mph
230 kmh

The contrast between the first half of the lap and the last three corners is clear to see from the gear-change data. Three first-gear corners end the lap after a wonderful succession of third- and fourth-gear sweepers

Redgate Corner

65 mph
100 kmh

35 mph
55 kmh

Melbourne Hairpin

RIDER'S VIEW Shakey Byrne

"Last year I thought I was going to have a terrible meeting, even my mates said I'd have a nightmare. But we underestimated the support I've got. When I got to the track it took me two hours to get to my motorhome. I ended up revving for the whole weekend, the fans turned the whole thing around for me. I've still got a photo of Kenny [Roberts, team owner] I took at Day of Champions in 1992, I must remember to take it and embarrass him with it this year."

ROUND **10**

SACHSENRING

31st July
SACHSENRING
www.sachsenring.de

This far eastern part of Germany used to be the epicentre of automotive engineering. The supercharged Auto Union race cars of the 1930s were built down the road in Chemnitz, Dr Walter Kaaden deduced the modern two-stroke from first principles in Zschopau, and many other historic companies flourished in the area. They raced their products on the Sachsenring street circuit which, after the Second World War, became the venue for the East German GP, an event that attracted up to a quarter of a million spectators. This is indeed an area steeped in motorsport history.

When the new Sachsenring was built it incorporated a small part of the old street circuit, but that is no longer used. The modification gave the track fresh character and created an epic section starting with the blind right-hander over a crest that leads to the downhill straight behind the paddock. In contrast, the first half of the track is as tight and twisty as it gets. The throttle's hardly opened in the first five corners, riders just shift gear and change direction. The last of those corners starts a sequence of six successive left-handers, all taken in third gear, which gives the tyre engineers something to think about.

Over the years clever modifications have turned the Sachsenring from a training facility into a track capable of producing top-class racing

Sachsenring

THE TRACK

Where is it?
The little town of Hohenstein-Ernstthal is right next to the track – the old street circuit used to go through it. The nearest big city is Dresden, 50 miles away.

Is it worth going to?
Yes, not least because this part of Europe still feels quite foreign. Local museums and nearby Colditz castle are must-see parts of the itinerary.

How do I get tickets?
This is the only race where I have seen fans beside the road with 'ticket wanted' signs, so don't go there without one!
Check out www.sachsenring.de

Where do I watch from?
Assuming you can get in, there are plenty of grandstands all round the track.

Where does the overtaking happen?
At the bottom of the fast hill is the favourite place, and you see the pass coming from way back. Turn 1 is also a good bet.

TV times
One hour ahead of UK time.

What should you eat and drink while watching the TV?
Real German beer made just from hops, spring water and barley, accompanied by a large wurst.

THE BIKES

Last year the Roman Emperor ruled in Germany as Hondas filled all three podium positions

Because of all the long corners, many taken at small throttle openings, smooth power delivery low down the rev range is vital here. The bikes are at full throttle for less than 10 per cent of the lap time, and a lot of the driving is done off the left side of the tyre on a track with hardly any camber. The rear suspension linkage rate will be more linear than usual to go with the flatter torque characteristics of the motor. This linkage should give a plusher ride over bumps in slow corners and improve traction on the way out. It should also help control the way a 250hp bike wants to wheelie all the time. To go with the linkage, the rear spring will be softer than usual to avoid working the rear tyre too hard on the bumps. Potential instability problems should be dialled out by damping settings. The front forks can also be relatively soft for all-round balance because of the lack of hard braking.

MotoGP @ SACHSENRING

2004 The highlight of Biaggi's year, with both pole position and the win, but it was still a good weekend for Rossi. He went top of the table despite finishing off the rostrum in fourth, after fighting with the Hondas of Barros and Hayden as well as with Max. Barros rode a heroic race to second, setting the fastest lap on shot tyres. Gibernau crashed early on, the Ducatis crashed too, and Melandri took out Abe in a dreadful-looking smash: both men were lucky to walk away from it.

2003 This was one of the greatest finishes ever: Gibernau took Rossi on the final corner after the Italian frittered away a two-second lead and then made a tactical error going into the last bend. Bayliss was third. The meeting is also remembered for Colin Edwards having to jump off his Aprilia after it burst into flames on the fastest part of the track and McWilliams coming within two thousandths of a second of pole on the two-stroke Modenas.

2002 Olivier Jacque took pole and it could have been a last win for the two-strokes if, three laps from home, Alex Barros hadn't attempted a desperate move at Turn 1 and taken them both down. This let Rossi in for a gift win. He'd been at the front for most of the race but lost ground after running wide and wouldn't have been able to do anything about the strokers if they'd stayed upright – their last chance of victory in MotoGP.

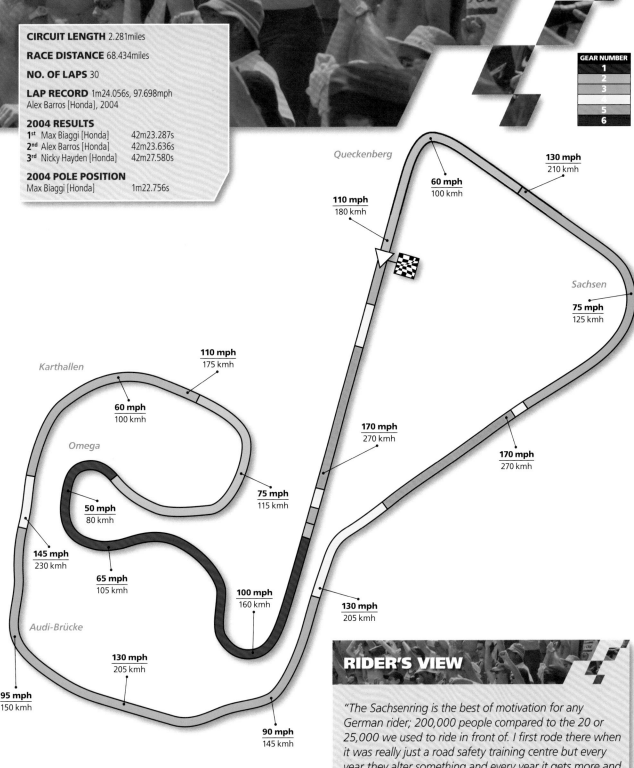

CIRCUIT LENGTH 2.281miles

RACE DISTANCE 68.434miles

NO. OF LAPS 30

LAP RECORD 1m24.056s, 97.698mph
Alex Barros [Honda], 2004

2004 RESULTS
1st Max Biaggi [Honda]   42m23.287s
2nd Alex Barros [Honda]   42m23.636s
3rd Nicky Hayden [Honda]   42m27.580s

2004 POLE POSITION
Max Biaggi [Honda]   1m22.756s

GEAR NUMBER	
1	
2	
3	
4	
5	
6	

Queckenberg

60 mph
100 kmh

130 mph
210 kmh

110 mph
180 kmh

Sachsen

75 mph
125 kmh

110 mph
175 kmh

Karthallen

60 mph
100 kmh

Omega

170 mph
270 kmh

50 mph
80 kmh

75 mph
115 kmh

170 mph
270 kmh

145 mph
230 kmh

65 mph
105 kmh

100 mph
160 kmh

Audi-Brücke

130 mph
205 kmh

130 mph
205 kmh

95 mph
150 kmh

90 mph
145 kmh

RIDER'S VIEW

"The Sachsenring is the best of motivation for any German rider; 200,000 people compared to the 20 or 25,000 we used to ride in front of. I first rode there when it was really just a road safety training centre but every year they alter something and every year it gets more and more like a real race track. It still suits a 125 or 250 more but I enjoy riding there. It's not easy to set a bike up. You spend a lot of time on the edge of the tyre at part throttle openings. It's about grip, about when you can open the throttle."

Alex Hofmann

Look how long a bike is on its side in third gear; it looks like nearly half a lap. Also, the throttle is hardly ever fully open; only ten percent of the time according to the data recorders

ROUND **11**

BRNO

28th August
AUTODROM BRNO
www.automotodrombrno.cz

Brno, the Czech Republic's second city, is in the south-east of the country not far from the Austrian border. The circuit is modern, wide, great to watch at and easily reached by car from Vienna or Prague. By UK standards, accommodation, food and drink are all cheap.

It's a great track to come back to after the summer break and one that has a habit of staging exciting races. A succession of second- and third-gear Esses go down into the bottom of a valley and back up again. The last two Esses are part of the power sapping uphill run back to the start/finish straight. The event attracts an increasingly large, cosmopolitan crowd, many of whom stay on the campsites around the track. In Cold War days the GP was held on a street circuit, part of which you drive down on the way from Brno to the track. The old pit buildings are still there and a hire-car lap of the old circuit is compulsory for all first-time visitors. However, the local cops have a zero-tolerance attitude to speeding, you are allowed no alcohol at all if you're driving, and there are radar traps and checks everywhere, so behave yourselves.

Great track, great crowd, great racing guaranteed; Brno has got a lot going for it if you fancy visiting a Continental race

Autodrom Brno

THE TRACK

Where is it?
The track is ten miles out of town, just off the motorway to Prague at Kyvalka. The circuit is actually named after the first president of Czechoslovakia, T. G. Masaryk.

Is it worth going to?
It's a great event at a great track – of course it's worth going to.

How do I get tickets?
If you want to sit in a specific grandstand go to www.automotodrombrno.cz otherwise pay on the day and sit on one of the enormous grass banks.

Where do I watch from?
The grassy hillsides that line the arena section at the bottom of the circuit are fine and full of atmosphere. Personally, I wouldn't bother with the small grandstand on the start/finish straight.

Where does the overtaking happen?
Everywhere; the track is so wide that even MotoGP bikes can pick different lines. Look out for that old truism 'slow in, fast out' on the ess bends, or someone making a move on the way in and baulking the other guy in the middle of the corner.

TV times
One hour ahead of UK time.

What should you eat and drink while watching the TV?
Utopenec s chlebem – sausage pickled with onions, a large chunk of bread and several local beers. Under no circumstances should you touch the watery American stuff, buy the real Czech article.

THE BIKES

Brno is not overly demanding on any specific area of chassis set-up. The target is good, stable turn-in character and easy changes in direction with lots of feel from both the front and rear. Weight bias is kept as neutral as possible to prevent the front being overworked at the midpoint of a turn while also ensuring good drive from the rear. Corner speed is the key to making up time here and, since the surface is relatively smooth and the top speeds only just nudge 300kph, straight-line stability can be sacrificed to achieve this objective.

A lower centre of gravity should control the rate of pitching and therefore help the bike's ability to change direction quickly. It should also reduce the risk of the front folding going into the downhill sweepers (caused when too much weight transfers onto the front tyre under deceleration). Softer springs front and rear will help feel and won't allow the rear shock to get overloaded as it would at a stop/go circuit with hard braking and acceleration.

Brno has given us some epic confrontations over the years, there's so much space even MotoGP bikes can use a variety of lines. It's one of the places that Bridgestone runners, like Kawasaki and this year Ducati, enjoy

MotoGP @ BRNO

2004 Sete Gibernau qualified on pole and led every lap, but it wasn't an easy win because Rossi and the Hondas of Hayden, Barros and Biaggi all broke away with him. Barros crashed while looking strong (again), Hayden was distracted by a Biaggi move on Rossi, lost concentration and crashed, and Max only got his nose in front of Rossi for a few yards. Interestingly, Tamada charged through late in the race to take fourth off Capirossi, and Hopkins was fastest in morning warm-up, so maybe Brno should be added to the list of tracks where Bridgestone tyres work well.

2003 This was an epic confrontation between Rossi and Gibernau, a gloves-off, tactics-free race decided on the last lap when Valentino didn't just overtake Sete, he broke Kato's lap record by the impossible margin of 0.7sec to take it under two minutes for the first time. The Ducatis were the only competition for the two front runners, Bayliss taking third but Capirossi stopping late on while looking threatening.

2002 This race ended Rossi's run of seven consecutive victories. The problem was tyre failure brought on by either a dodgy slipper clutch or a power-up modification that Michelin hadn't been warned about – depending on who you listened to. Biaggi took Yamaha's first victory in MotoGP on one of his favourite circuits and Daijiro Kato finished second in his first ride on the RC211V.

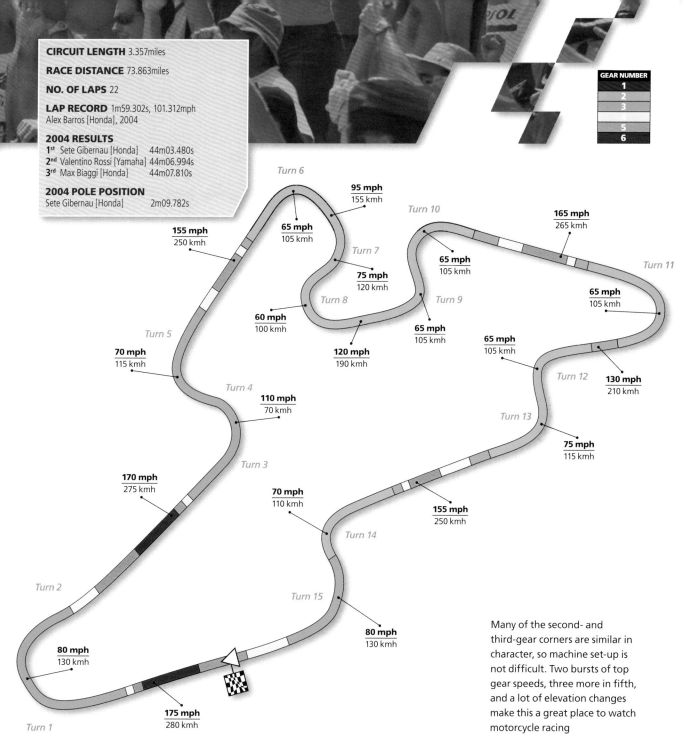

CIRCUIT LENGTH 3.357miles

RACE DISTANCE 73.863miles

NO. OF LAPS 22

LAP RECORD 1m59.302s, 101.312mph
Alex Barros [Honda], 2004

2004 RESULTS
1st Sete Gibernau [Honda]   44m03.480s
2nd Valentino Rossi [Yamaha]   44m06.994s
3rd Max Biaggi [Honda]   44m07.810s

2004 POLE POSITION
Sete Gibernau [Honda]   2m09.782s

GEAR NUMBER
1
2
3
4
5
6

Turn 6

95 mph 155 kmh

Turn 10

165 mph 265 kmh

155 mph 250 kmh

65 mph 105 kmh

Turn 7

Turn 11

65 mph 105 kmh

75 mph 120 kmh

Turn 8

Turn 9

65 mph 105 kmh

60 mph 100 kmh

65 mph 105 kmh

Turn 5

65 mph 105 kmh

130 mph 210 kmh

70 mph 115 kmh

120 mph 190 kmh

65 mph 105 kmh

Turn 12

Turn 4

110 mph 70 kmh

Turn 13

Turn 3

70 mph 110 kmh

75 mph 115 kmh

170 mph 275 kmh

Turn 14

155 mph 250 kmh

Turn 2

Turn 15

80 mph 130 kmh

80 mph 130 kmh

175 mph 280 kmh

Turn 1

Many of the second- and third-gear corners are similar in character, so machine set-up is not difficult. Two bursts of top gear speeds, three more in fifth, and a lot of elevation changes make this a great place to watch motorcycle racing

RIDER'S VIEW *Max Biaggi*

"Brno is wide, so you can use a lot of different lines. It's up to the rider to use the best line every lap depending on the situation, which makes it really interesting. Machine set-up is very important wherever you go, but you need to work especially hard at choosing the correct front tyre for this race; front-end grip is so important because there are many off-camber corners. You also need stable tyres, so the bike doesn't move around when you're at high lean angles, so you can get good drive off the corners. The track is quite bumpy too, so you can sometimes get chatter."

ROUND **12**
MOTEGI

18th September
TWIN RING MOTEGI
www.twinring.co.jp

Twin Ring Motegi

Out in the sticks, 60 miles north-east of Tokyo, Honda built a state-of-the-art oval circuit to demonstrate their commitment to American car racing and to test their Indy racers on. Fortunately, they incorporated a road circuit as well and it's on the doorstep of Honda's Tochigi R&D centre. The result is a thoroughly modern facility with an almost perfect surface and good safety – apart from the start, obviously. Most of the corners are short, constant-radius right-angles that do little to test a rider. However, the second part of the track – the bit outside the oval – has a fast set of ess bends, a sneaky hairpin and a top-speed run downhill to the hardest braking effort of the lap at the imaginatively named 90-degree corner.

Last year Makoto Tamada dominated the Japanese GP using Bridgestone tyres. How will he fair on Michelins this time?

The other great attraction of Motegi is the Collection Hall, Honda's company museum. It contains examples of every machine the company has made, including mythical beasts such as Mike Hailwood's six-cylinder 250 and the five-cylinder 21,500rpm 125 of 1966 with which Honda attempted to stem the two-stroke tide. You can even stare through a plate-glass window into the workshop where the next treasure is being restored.

THE TRACK

Where is it?
Motegi is half way between Mito and Utsunomiya and about three hours' drive north of Tokyo, even though the distance involved is only about 70 miles.

Is it worth going to?
Japan isn't a different country, it's like a different planet. Prepare for severe culture shock and don't forget to set aside plenty of time to visit the museum.

How do I get tickets?
Go to www.twinring.co.jp before you fly. Because access to the track is by tiny country roads the authorities cap the number of tickets, so even though the grandstands aren't full it doesn't mean you can get in on the day.

Where do I watch from?
Most fans sit in the giant grandstand opposite the pits. It looks out over the oval track's straight and is high enough to give you a panoramic view of nearly everything. You'd want to nip round to the stand alongside the braking area for 90-degree corner at some point, because that's the closest you can get to the action.

Where does the overtaking happen?
There are at least four places where a pass on the brakes is not just possible but likely. At 90-degree corner the other guy doesn't have a chance to get back before the start/finish line. Although Elias did manage to get Melandri coming out of the last chicane in 250s...

TV times
Nine hours ahead of UK time.

What should you eat and drink while watching the TV?
A bowl of noodles and a cup of green tea.

MotoGP @ MOTEGI

2004 The second first-bend pile-up in consecutive years saw Capirossi skittle all four Americans and Max Biaggi. Slow-starting Rossi and Tamada avoided the melee and fought out the race between them, Makoto (on Bridgestones in '04) making good his pre-race threat to take revenge on the Italian for humiliating him two weeks earlier in Portugal. To the joy of the local fans, Shinya Nakano took Kawasaki's first MotoGP rostrum in third place.

2003 John Hopkins initiated a first-lap crash that took Checa and Bayliss out, and hampered Edwards; Race Direction decided to ban him from the next race. Rossi made a mistake, as he'd done in Barcelona, and had to try to catch a fast-disappearing leader. This time it was a faultless Max Biaggi, who couldn't be caught. Everyone thought Tamada was third after putting a hard pass on Gibernau a couple of corners from home, but it was called a foul and he was disqualified, so Nicky Hayden inherited his first rostrum finish in GPs without standing on the rostrum.

2002 Alex Barros got his first ride on a four-stroke and promptly used it to beat Rossi (who had sewn up the title at the previous race), but he had to set a new lap record last time round to do it. Loris Capirossi, Barros's team-mate, rode a heroic race to third on the two-stroke Honda.

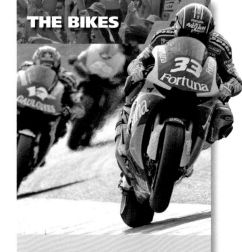

THE BIKES

The things you don't need here are too much weight transfer going into a corner and vicious power delivery coming out of it. As the corners are very short, these two phases arrive very close together. Furthermore, the bike is on its side for a very short period of time so the rear tyre doesn't have much time to get any heat in it.

To control fore and aft pitching, the rear of the bike will be set slightly lower and the front slightly higher than at other circuits. This should keep things stable under braking and stop the rear wheel coming off the ground. The front fork springs will need a high rate, but the damping won't have to cater for any serious bumps while the front forks are compressed.

The rear shock, on the other hand, will run a slightly softer spring with high preload. This should deliver the feel and consistency needed under power and prevent the bike from squatting to the point where it runs wide or even wheelies. The worry is that these settings will let the rear shock 'pump' through its stroke driving out of slow corners.

Two years running the first corner at Motegi has been the scene of a mass pile up. Last year Capirossi was the instigator; 2003 culprit Hopkins was the main victim

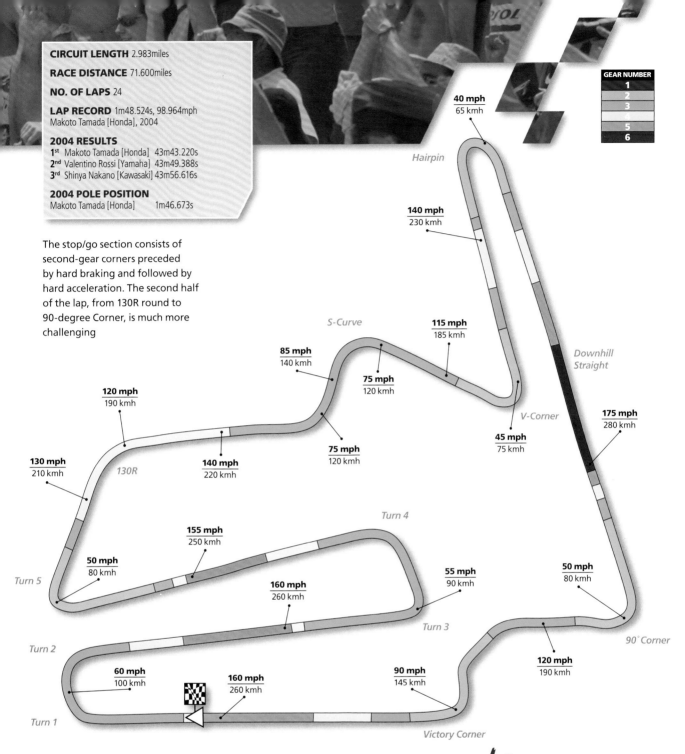

CIRCUIT LENGTH 2.983miles

RACE DISTANCE 71.600miles

NO. OF LAPS 24

LAP RECORD 1m48.524s, 98.964mph
Makoto Tamada [Honda], 2004

2004 RESULTS
1st Makoto Tamada [Honda] 43m43.220s
2nd Valentino Rossi [Yamaha] 43m49.388s
3rd Shinya Nakano [Kawasaki] 43m56.616s

2004 POLE POSITION
Makoto Tamada [Honda] 1m46.673s

GEAR NUMBER
1	
2	
3	
4	
5	
6	

The stop/go section consists of second-gear corners preceded by hard braking and followed by hard acceleration. The second half of the lap, from 130R round to 90-degree Corner, is much more challenging

40 mph 65 kmh

Hairpin

140 mph 230 kmh

Downhill Straight

S-Curve

115 mph 185 kmh

85 mph 140 kmh

75 mph 120 kmh

V-Corner

120 mph 190 kmh

75 mph 120 kmh

45 mph 75 kmh

175 mph 280 kmh

130 mph 210 kmh

130R

140 mph 220 kmh

Turn 4

155 mph 250 kmh

50 mph 80 kmh

160 mph 260 kmh

55 mph 90 kmh

50 mph 80 kmh

Turn 5

Turn 3

90° Corner

Turn 2

60 mph 100 kmh

160 mph 260 kmh

90 mph 145 kmh

120 mph 190 kmh

Turn 1

Victory Corner

RIDER'S VIEW — *Makoto Tamada*

"Tyres are an important factor for this GP, I made the right choice last year which is why I won the race. My favourite turn is the right hander at the end of the back straight. Other riders have told me that it's like I disappear there! I am very confident at this corner and can always attack there. The track is not difficult, there are no secrets, not like Mugello for instance. If you stay concentrated and don't worry about anybody else it is difficult for an opponent to pass you. It's the same with the bike, if you stay concentrated and don't make any mistakes there should be no reliability problems with it or the tyres."

ROUND **13**

SEPANG

25th September
SEPANG F1 CIRCUIT
www.malaysiangp.com.my

Malaysia is a heady mixture of indigenous Malay, Chinese and Indian cultures with European influences. The official religion is Islam but there are large Hindu and Buddhist communities too, and everyone seems to get along pretty well. Kuala Lumpur, the capital, is a thriving business and financial centre with the once-highest building in the world, the Petronas Twin Towers, at its centre. There are beaches and islands nearby – the most famous is Lankawi – if you fancy a holiday in the sun.

Sepang F1 Circuit

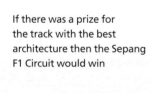

If there was a prize for the track with the best architecture then the Sepang F1 Circuit would win

The track is modern, wide, with fantastic facilities, and was built to bring Formula 1 to Malaysia. The lap starts and ends with long straights either side of a central plaza that contains the majority of the seating, although there are other giant grandstands out in the country. A variety of corners, including a couple of testing fast sweepers, make the circuit much more than a couple of interconnected drag races. Last year there was a respectable crowd too, the Rossi effect in action in the Far East.

THE TRACK

Where is it?
About an hour's drive south of Kuala Lumpur, near the KL International Airport.

Is it worth going to?
Yes, Kuala Lumpur is a great city to visit or you could make the GP part of an Asian holiday.

How do I get tickets?
No problem, just turn up on the day.

Where do I watch from?
Just about everyone watches in the giant stands either side of the central plaza, where all the facilities – catering, trade stands – are located. There is a giant screen down towards Turn 1. Seats on the other side of the plaza give you a panoramic view of a large section of the track, although the temperature might dissuade you from walking about too much.

Where does the overtaking happen?
On the brakes at the end of either straight is the favourite tactic, but there are other possibilities, as Rossi showed last year. The track is so wide that even the MotoGP bikes can make a variety of lines work while the smaller classes can get through anywhere three or more abreast.

TV times
Eight hours ahead of UK time.

What should you eat and drink while watching the TV?
It has to be Malaysia's national dish, which is satay, accompanied by a Tiger Beer.

THE BIKES

Both Yamaha and Honda have won here; the big surprise is that Ducati have never figured in the results despite lots of testing.

Sepang doesn't put any particular demands on machinery thanks in part to the smooth condition of the surface. The heavy braking at the end of the twin straights and high corner-entry speeds demand excellent stability on the brakes and good turn-in characteristics. For once front tyres need some attention as the width of the track means long entry phases to the big sweepers. To help cater for both, the suspension balance will be targeted towards the neutral feel used at Motegi. Stiffer front springs will be used to cope with the extreme braking and cornering forces, with the bike's attitude controlled by the spring preload. Softer damper settings will give some feel. The rear shock will also use a high rate spring, but the damping needs to be smooth to give the riders the feel needed to get the power down hard and predictably in conditions that can melt a rear tyre in a matter of laps.

Rossi got his settings so spot-on last year that he used a softer tyre than most of the other riders and still won.

MotoGP @ SEPANG

2004 Rossi took his revenge for the slights – real or imagined – of Qatar the week before, when he'd been sent to the back of the grid and subsequently crashed. He arrived at Sepang deeply disgruntled with Honda in general and Gibernau in particular, and proceeded to grind the opposition into the dust. Valentino started from pole and was briefly held up by Barros before disappearing into the heat haze to win by over three-and-a-half seconds, setting a new lap record on the way and almost guaranteeing that he'd retain his title.

Biaggi took a fighting second place from the third row of the grid; Gibernau had a nightmare race, finishing sixth with four other Hondas in front of him.

2003 Rossi retained his title with a win over Gibernau despite only needing to finish second. Sete led early on and when Rossi came past he refused to give up and was only beaten by a couple of seconds at the flag. Biaggi was a distant third.

2002 Biaggi won for Yamaha after Rossi took pole-man Barros wide at the last corner while trying an outbraking manoeuvre which let his team-mate Ukawa past. Leader Biaggi made good his escape and afterwards Rossi had a go at the Japanese rider for racing with him as he tried to catch the Roman.

Valentino's post-race stunt last year was a reference to events the previous week in Qatar

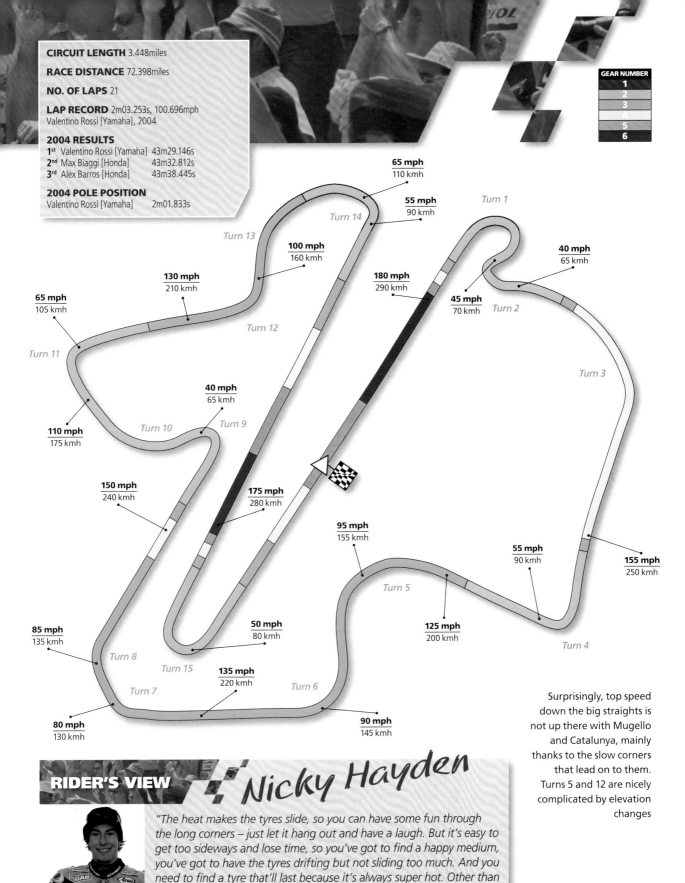

CIRCUIT LENGTH 3.448miles

RACE DISTANCE 72.398miles

NO. OF LAPS 21

LAP RECORD 2m03.253s, 100.696mph
Valentino Rossi [Yamaha], 2004

2004 RESULTS
1st Valentino Rossi [Yamaha] 43m29.146s
2nd Max Biaggi [Honda] 43m32.812s
3rd Alex Barros [Honda] 43m38.445s

2004 POLE POSITION
Valentino Rossi [Yamaha] 2m01.833s

GEAR NUMBER

| 1 |
| 2 |
| 3 |
| 4 |
| 5 |
| 6 |

65 mph 110 kmh — Turn 14

55 mph 90 kmh

Turn 1

Turn 13

100 mph 160 kmh

180 mph 290 kmh

40 mph 65 kmh

45 mph 70 kmh — **Turn 2**

130 mph 210 kmh

Turn 12

65 mph 105 kmh

Turn 11

Turn 3

110 mph 175 kmh

40 mph 65 kmh

Turn 10 Turn 9

150 mph 240 kmh

175 mph 280 kmh

95 mph 155 kmh

55 mph 90 kmh

155 mph 250 kmh

85 mph 135 kmh

Turn 8

50 mph 80 kmh

125 mph 200 kmh

Turn 4

Turn 15 **135 mph** 220 kmh Turn 5

Turn 7 Turn 6

80 mph 130 kmh

90 mph 145 kmh

Surprisingly, top speed down the big straights is not up there with Mugello and Catalunya, mainly thanks to the slow corners that lead on to them. Turns 5 and 12 are nicely complicated by elevation changes

RIDER'S VIEW *Nicky Hayden*

"The heat makes the tyres slide, so you can have some fun through the long corners – just let it hang out and have a laugh. But it's easy to get too sideways and lose time, so you've got to find a happy medium, you've got to have the tyres drifting but not sliding too much. And you need to find a tyre that'll last because it's always super hot. Other than that it's not like it's a real complex or challenging track, in fact I find it a little featureless because there's no elevation changes and nothing that makes you go 'Wow, that's cool'."

ROUND **14**
LOSAIL

1st October

**LOSAIL INTERNATIONAL
RACETRACK**
www.qmmf.com

The tiny Emirate of Qatar sees sport as one way of engaging with the outside world, hosting important tennis tournaments on the PTA and WTA tours, and paying all-time great footballers considerable amounts to play in the domestic league – Frank Leboeuf and Gabriel Batistuta were visitors to the MotoGP paddock last year. It will also host the Asian Games in 2006, and there is a racing yacht in round-the-world races called Doha 2006 just to underline the fact.

Motorcycle racing is another sport which is seen as useful in advertising the country of Qatar and helping Qatari society open up to the outside world in a positive way.

All these influences make for a GP like no other. The track is interesting and mercifully free of chicanes, the

teams and media have excellent facilities, and it's all on a human scale, with nothing grandiose or overblown. There's more bling at Mugello.

The one thing there isn't is a crowd and those who were there last year seemed to be expatriate workers, mainly from Europe and Australia, although I did bump into fans who had flown in specially from Saudi Arabia and Oman. Note that, like Assen, this is a Saturday race.

Losail International Racetrack

The Losail track is just one of a number of world class sporting facilities built in Qatar in recent years

THE TRACK

Where is it?
Losail is about 20 miles outside Doha, the capital of Qatar, in totally flat and otherwise empty country. It isn't even desert, just barren rocky terrain.

Is it worth going to?
It's a totally different experience from any other Grand Prix meeting. If you do go, remember that you will be visiting a largely traditional Moslem country and act accordingly. Hotel prices and food can be on the expensive side.

How do I get tickets?
No problems – there were only a few hundred people in the stand last year – but go to www.qmmf.com for further information.

Where do I watch from?
There is only the one grandstand, alongside the main straight. Don't underestimate the effects of the sun; drink plenty of water and keep in the shade.

Where does the overtaking happen?
With a kilometre-long straight, slipstreaming followed by a move on the brakes at Turn 1 is the favourite. There are other places: Turn 6, the slowest on the track, sees some action, and it is possible to steal someone's line through the interlinked sections. The final turn is for desperate moves only.

TV times
Three hours ahead of UK time.

What should you eat and drink while watching the TV?
Barbecued lamb and saffron rice followed by the stickiest, honey-soaked pastries you can find.

MotoGP @ LOSAIL

2004 What didn't happen on MotoGP's first visit to the Middle East? Rossi and Biaggi were sent to the back of the grid because their crews illegally doctored their starting positions. Then Rossi crashed in the race while Gibernau won, closing the gap at the top of the table to 14 points with two races left.

Many of the problems were caused by the new track being very green and covered with a layer of fine dust: a racing line did emerge by race day, but riders were in trouble if they got off it. This, and the featureless terrain which meant riders couldn't find any braking markers, was responsible for many excursions into the giant gravel traps over the weekend.

Rossi's race crash happened after he charged up to eighth at the end of the first lap, having started from 22nd. Four laps later he used all of the track plus the rumble strip and more. Unfortunately for him, it was Astroturf not grass at the side of the track and he highsided immediately. That left Gibernau to win from team-mate Edwards with Xaus taking his first MotoGP podium – and Ducati's first of the year – once luckless pole-man Checa had been put out by fuel-pump failure.

THE BIKES

The circuit is very technical so it should be possible for a team to improve things dramatically over race weekend. As everywhere, you need balance but the key here is to build the rider's confidence in his ability to tip the bike into a corner and come out the other side on his wheels.

Last year the track was brand new, very green, very dusty and very slippery. Back in March this year the fastest laps at a test session were approximately three seconds faster than in the actual race last year. That is such an improvement that you might as well be at a different track as far as bike settings are concerned.

So will the data from those tests be relevant? Not really, because compared to March, the track and ambient temperatures will be 20 or 30 degrees higher in late September when practice starts for real.

In effect no-one will have much in the way of useable data. Expect most race engineers to size up the problems pretty quickly but don't be surprised if one or two are lost for a session or two.

James Haydon stood in for Kurtis Roberts at Proton last year and got the bike's best result of the season. Here he is passed by eventual winner Gibernau

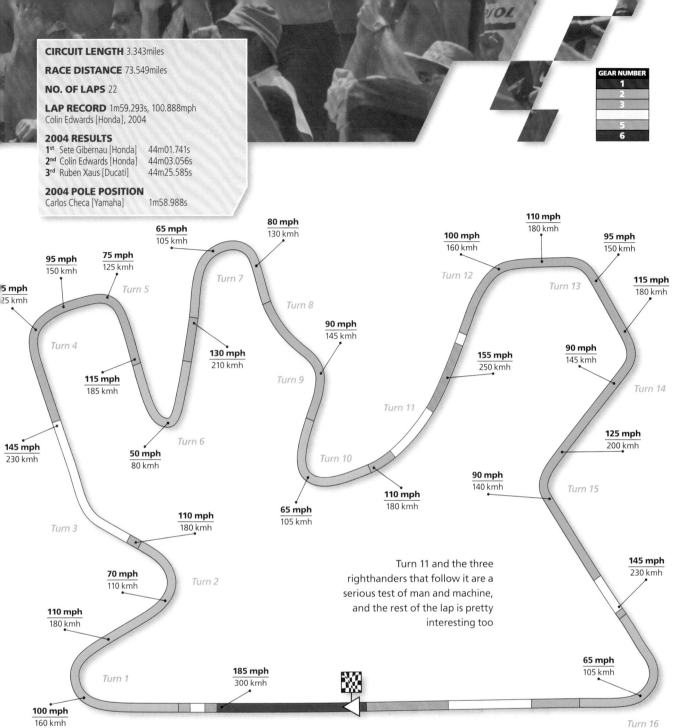

CIRCUIT LENGTH 3.343miles

RACE DISTANCE 73.549miles

NO. OF LAPS 22

LAP RECORD 1m59.293s, 100.888mph
Colin Edwards [Honda], 2004

2004 RESULTS
1st Sete Gibernau [Honda]   44m01.741s
2nd Colin Edwards [Honda]   44m03.056s
3rd Ruben Xaus [Ducati]   44m25.585s

2004 POLE POSITION
Carlos Checa [Yamaha]   1m58.988s

GEAR NUMBER
1
2
3
5
6

65 mph / 105 kmh
80 mph / 130 kmh
Turn 7
Turn 8
75 mph / 125 kmh
95 mph / 150 kmh
5 mph / 25 kmh
Turn 5
100 mph / 160 kmh
Turn 12
110 mph / 180 kmh
95 mph / 150 kmh
Turn 13
115 mph / 180 kmh
Turn 4
130 mph / 210 kmh
90 mph / 145 kmh
Turn 9
155 mph / 250 kmh
90 mph / 145 kmh
115 mph / 185 kmh
Turn 11
Turn 14
145 mph / 230 kmh
Turn 6
50 mph / 80 kmh
Turn 10
90 mph / 140 kmh
125 mph / 200 kmh
65 mph / 105 kmh
110 mph / 180 kmh
Turn 15
Turn 3
110 mph / 180 kmh
145 mph / 230 kmh
70 mph / 110 kmh
Turn 2
Turn 11 and the three
righthanders that follow it are a
serious test of man and machine,
and the rest of the lap is pretty
interesting too
110 mph / 180 kmh
Turn 1
185 mph / 300 kmh
65 mph / 105 kmh
100 mph / 160 kmh
Turn 16

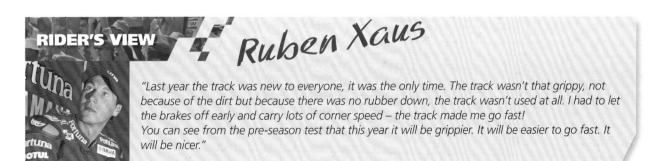

RIDER'S VIEW · Ruben Xaus

"Last year the track was new to everyone, it was the only time. The track wasn't that grippy, not because of the dirt but because there was no rubber down, the track wasn't used at all. I had to let the brakes off early and carry lots of corner speed – the track made me go fast!
You can see from the pre-season test that this year it will be grippier. It will be easier to go fast. It will be nicer."

ROUND **15**

PHILLIP ISLAND

16th October

PHILLIP ISLAND
www.phillipislandcircuit.com.au

Phillip Island

Probably the finest race track in the world and a real test of man and machine: no circuit is harder on tyres than Phillip Island thanks to the long corners that are entered at speed and powered round. Despite the two slow turns there is no part of this circuit that is anything less than mind-boggling. The top-speed run down to Turn 1, with the ocean as a backdrop, the run out of Siberia up to Lukey Heights where Rossi made that impossible pass last year, the scarily fast succession of lefts that ends the lap and sends bikes plunging back down the Gardner Straight – all are fascinating and awe-inspiring in the true meaning of that phrase.

Phillip Island itself is primarily a holiday resort and weekend retreat for affluent Melbournites; in fact, it is a dead-ringer for a small British seaside resort. The Victoria police seem intent on not allowing anyone to escape from the campsites or to do something as scurrilous as opening a can of beer on the street,

When the sun shines Phillip Island is glorious, but that stretch of water is the Bass Straight and the next land you hit is Tasmania. If the weather turns bad the Island can, to quote Barry Sheene, be the home of hypothermia

but the organisers put on a great show at the track with high quality support races, stunt riders, supercross demos and a goodly number of trade stands. But the only thing that really matters is that glorious ribbon of tarmac.

THE TRACK

Where is it?
Phillip Island is 80 miles south-east of Melbourne, just off the South Gippsland Highway.

Is it worth going to?
Some time in your life you must see a GP at Phillip Island. The only other highlight of the Island is the Fairy Penguin Parade, so make visiting this race track part of an extended tour of a fascinating country.

How do I get tickets?
Go to www.phillipislandcircuit.co.au for info. You should be able to pay on the day, but would you travel that far without a ticket?

Where do I watch from?
Everywhere. There isn't one part of this place that doesn't repay study.

Where does the overtaking happen?
Again, everywhere: Rossi proved that last year. You'll see slipstreaming down the straight, braking duels at Honda and MG corners and, if you're very lucky, the type of move that Rossi pulled off last year and Hayden managed twice the year before.

TV times
Ten hours ahead of UK time.

What should you eat and drink while watching the TV?
Informal: a pie and a can of ready-mixed bourbon and coke (honest!). Formal: something from the fusion school of cuisine accompanied by a bottle of Hunter Valley red.

THE BIKES

The fast flowing nature of Phillip Island allows riders with 250 horsepower underneath them the rare opportunity of attacking a circuit. Bikes need to have good linear acceleration and turning ability rather than braking stability as the only hard braking comes at Honda corner. The key is a high average speed, not top speed, through the long, sweeping high-speed corners, which means a motor mapped for top-end power with progressive delivery.

The rear shock has to use softish spring rate to give the rider feel, but with a reasonable amount of preload to prevent rear-end squat. The front forks will mimic the rear set-up to ensure overall balanced, neutral geometry. Go too hard and the front will become vague in its feedback (and at the high speeds and lean angles here that is not a comfortable feeling); go too soft and it will just feel sloppy. Getting the power down while leaned well over at speed is the key to a fast lap time, with the exit of the final turn being particularly vital. The momentum carried through here can make the difference between winning and losing.

MotoGP @ PHILLIP ISLAND

2004 Rossi won the race and the title after race-long combat with Gibernau. He only had to follow Sete home to be champion again. Instead, the lead changed three times on the last lap: Rossi went in front at Turn 1, then outbraked himself at Honda only to go round the outside at Lukey Heights to put himself on the inside at MG: wonderful to watch. Ducati finally had something to smile about with a fighting third place from Capirossi.

2003 Rossi made a pass under a yellow flag and received a ten-second penalty as per the newly amended post-Donington rule. On lap 11 his crew signalled him that he was ten seconds down. As he was leading at the time it took him a while to realise what had happened but, once he'd absorbed the info, he unleashed his full talent in anger, maybe for the first time. He won the race by 5 seconds from Capirossi. Anyone who had ever doubted Valentino Rossi had all their questions answered. Nicky Hayden put consecutive passes on Ukawa and Gibernau at Lukey Heights to stand on the rostrum for the second time.

2002 McWilliams took the final two-stroke pole on the Proton triple, Rossi won the race from a persistent Barros with Ukawa a distant third, and Barry Sheene visited a GP paddock for the last time. He joined the riders in a parade of open cars and got a bigger cheer then even Rossi or local hero McCoy.

Phillip Island 2004 was a microcosm of the season as a whole, with Rossi and Gibernau in close combat for the whole race

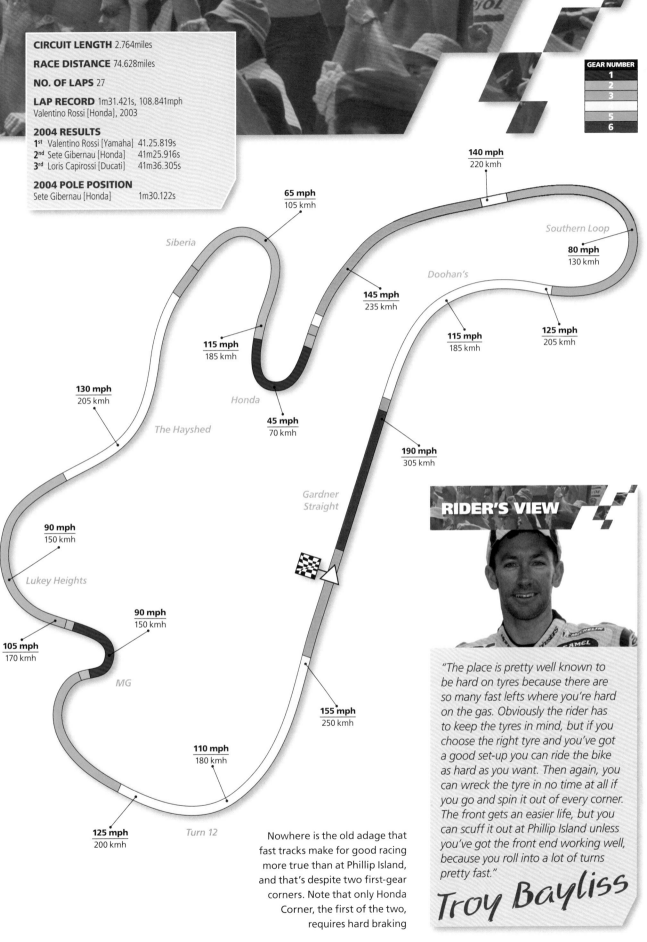

CIRCUIT LENGTH 2.764miles

RACE DISTANCE 74.628miles

NO. OF LAPS 27

LAP RECORD 1m31.421s, 108.841mph
Valentino Rossi [Honda], 2003

2004 RESULTS
1st Valentino Rossi [Yamaha]   41.25.819s
2nd Sete Gibernau [Honda]   41m25.916s
3rd Loris Capirossi [Ducati]   41m36.305s

2004 POLE POSITION
Sete Gibernau [Honda]   1m30.122s

GEAR NUMBER
1
2
3
4
5
6

140 mph
220 kmh

Southern Loop

80 mph
130 kmh

65 mph
105 kmh

Siberia

Doohan's

145 mph
235 kmh

125 mph
205 kmh

115 mph
185 kmh

115 mph
185 kmh

130 mph
205 kmh

The Hayshed

Honda

45 mph
70 kmh

190 mph
305 kmh

Gardner
Straight

RIDER'S VIEW

90 mph
150 kmh

Lukey Heights

90 mph
150 kmh

105 mph
170 kmh

MG

155 mph
250 kmh

110 mph
180 kmh

125 mph
200 kmh

Turn 12

"The place is pretty well known to be hard on tyres because there are so many fast lefts where you're hard on the gas. Obviously the rider has to keep the tyres in mind, but if you choose the right tyre and you've got a good set-up you can ride the bike as hard as you want. Then again, you can wreck the tyre in no time at all if you go and spin it out of every corner. The front gets an easier life, but you can scuff it out at Phillip Island unless you've got the front end working well, because you roll into a lot of turns pretty fast."

Troy Bayliss

Nowhere is the old adage that fast tracks make for good racing more true than at Phillip Island, and that's despite two first-gear corners. Note that only Honda Corner, the first of the two, requires hard braking

ROUND **16**

ISTANBUL

30th October
ISTANBUL RACING CIRCUIT
www.formula1-istanbul.com

The Turkish government regards this circuit as an important project, and it certainly looks as if they are putting together a good facility. When Bernie Ecclestone visited to see how construction was progressing he said, with typical brevity, that it was going to be 'the best'.

The F1 cars go there in August (the race is on the 21st) so you may have to watch TV to form some preliminary ideas of the place. However, just from the scale of the building works and the track map, you can see that the circuit has variety and that kink in the back straight brings back memories of the 130R corner at Suzuka. The circuit has been planned on four levels with significant gradients linking the sections. Worryingly, plans for the future include a kart track inside the main track: never a good idea when bike racers have some spare time on their hands.

The F1 guys reckon they'll be hitting over 185mph down into Turn 12 on the 720-metre straight, the longest on the track. As the bikes generally have higher top speeds than the cars, but get round the corner much slower, reckon on a top speed of around 175mph.

The main grandstand you can see in the aerial picture will hold 30,000 spectators. Further temporary stands and grass bankings will increase capacity to over 155,000.

They've already shifted a lot of earth and you can see what an impressive facility it's going to be

RIDER'S VIEW

Kevin Schwantz & Randy Mamola

"How long is it? Over five kilometres? And wide, too. Over 20 metres in places. Turn 1 could be a little sticky but the run through the next four corners looks pretty neat. And it's got a fast section out the back."

"Listen, you just know it's going to be good. Look at the brand new tracks we've been to recently, they're all good. This one looks pretty interesting for the riders as well. Kevin's right, that righthander out the back will be fun."

Istanbul Racing Circuit

THE TRACK

Turn 9
Turn 10
Turn 8
Turn 7
Turn 11
Turn 4
Turn 5 & 6
Turn 12 & 13
Turn 2
Turn 3
Turn 14
Turn 1

Where is it?
Over the Bosphorus on the Asian side of the city, four miles from the Kurtkoy junction on the Istanbul to Ankara motorway and close to the new Sabiha Gokcen Istanbul international airport. That's over 50 miles from central Istanbul.

Is it worth going to?
Istanbul is unique in being the only city to be on two continents, and it's got more historical and cultural sights than anywhere this side of Rome or Venice. You'd go just to ride over the bridge that links Europe and Asia.

How do I get tickets?
The website seems very useful so keep an eye on it, but the place is going to be so big you can't imagine not beng able to buy a ticket on the day.

TV times
Two hours ahead of UK time.

What should you eat and drink while watching the TV?
A nice selction of mezze snacks, probably some grilled aubergine with yoghurt or humous with pitta bread.Drink mint tea or wickedly strong coffee.

ROUND **17**

RICARDO TORMO

6th November
CIRCUITO RICARDO TORMO
www.circuitvalencia.com

Valencia has now become the traditional venue for the last race of the year – a full house packed into the huge grandstands that overlook the only stadium track in the calendar. All the action takes place in a space so small that every spectator can see all of the time. Many fans stay in nearby Cheste, which gets very lively on Saturday night when, in accordance with local tradition, giant effigies of the top Spanish racers are burnt – it's about the biggest compliment you can receive in this corner of Spain.

Valencia itself is Spain's third city, with superb seafood restaurants in the port area, a splendid old town and breathtaking modern architecture in the cultural quarter. It's also Spain's fireworks capital, so you'll see a chap in traditional costume helping the winner of each race light the celebratory tracas, strings of firecrackers that sound like machine-guns only much louder. The display at the end of the day's racing boasts more firepower than the army of a medium-sized country.

So many fans and so many corners all crammed into such a small space

Circuito Ricardo Tormo

THE TRACK

Where is it?
About 20 miles from the city centre, just off the motorway to Madrid. The nearest town of any size is Cheste. Handily, Valencia airport is only a couple of junctions back down the motorway to the city and Alicante is a few hours' drive away.

Is it worth going to?
It's a unique event at a unique (to MotoGP) venue, and the atmosphere is very special. There's even the Spanish version of Day of Champions on the Thursday.

How do I get tickets?
This is another race that I wouldn't travel to without a ticket, although you stand a chance of buying one on the gate during qualifying: www.circuitvalencia.com

Where do I watch from?
The Grada Norte Amarillo (Yellow North Stand) between the first and second turns fills up first, then Blue, Green and Red along the west of the track from where you get a great view of the infield. If you can't get a seat there's always the hillside above the stands.

Where does the overtaking happen?
Slipstream down to Turn 1 and then outbrake is a favourite move, and Turn 2 also gets a lot of use, but the last corner is only for the brave and the desperate.

TV times
One hour ahead of UK time.

What should you eat and drink while watching the TV?
It has to be paella, Valencia's speciality. A crisp white Rioja should wash it down nicely.

Valentino says he doesn't like the track but he's won there; Nicky likes it but has fallen both times he's raced there

THE BIKES

Valencia has helpful cambers and an abrasive surface, but its slightly undulating terrain means that its many stop-and-go 90-degree corners, bumps and generally tight layout test the front end severely. Teams will be chasing security in this area, followed by stability on the brakes without sacrificing the agility to deal with a circuit that is more suited to a 250 than a MotoGP four-stroke.

The more linear characteristics of the new generation of 'big bang' engines give riders and tyres less of a hard time than in previous years, making it easier to get on the power earlier in the turn and with more confidence. This is essential in the final turn, which also happens to be the only one without positive camber.

As at other circuits with a lot of hard braking, the front end will be set slightly higher than usual and the rear lower. As usual, the problem at the rear is eliminating squat without inducing oversteer or making the bike too prone to wheelie.

MotoGP @ VALENCIA

2004 Rossi crowned his first season at Yamaha with his ninth win of the year after Tamada led but ran into tyre problems. Biaggi had been in front of Rossi but was taken wide by an errant Gibernau, who had a bad weekend. Nevertheless, Max took second and the fastest lap with Troy Bayliss, in his last ride for Ducati, making it to his first podium of 2004.

2003 This was Rossi's last race for Honda. He and the RCV had a special Austin Powers paint scheme for the day, designed by the winner of a magazine competition – and he topped it off with an Afro wig on the rostrum. Valentino dealt with some early pressure from Gibernau, who finished second, while Capirossi came some way back in third to take his sixth podium of the year for Ducati.

2002 Barros had his fourth ride on the Honda four-stroke and made it two wins, a second and one third place from the last four races of the year. This time it was top spot, the Brazilian veteran beating Rossi in a last-lap braking duel. Alex took the lead at Turn 1, ran wide and let Valentino alongside, but then won after a decisive late, late move on the brakes at Turn 2. Biaggi was third to wrap up second in the championship.

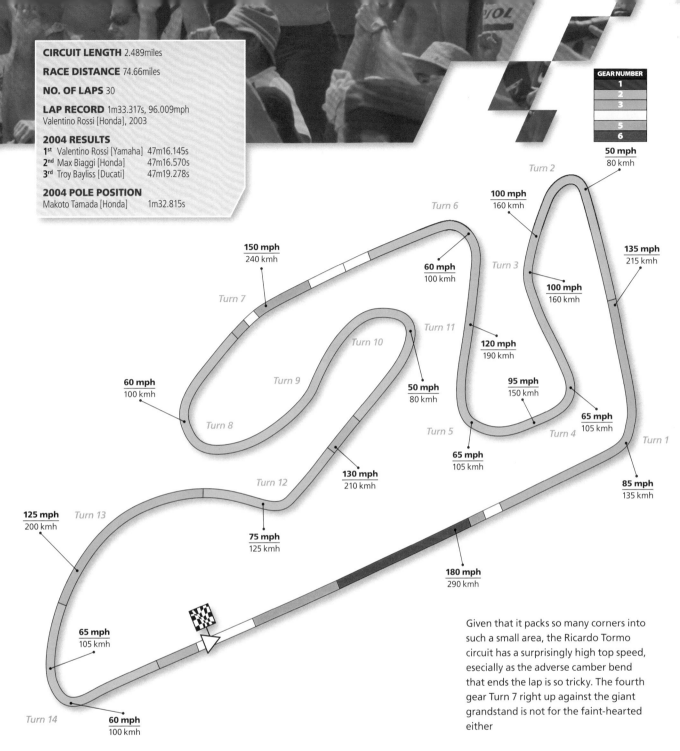

CIRCUIT LENGTH 2.489miles

RACE DISTANCE 74.66miles

NO. OF LAPS 30

LAP RECORD 1m33.317s, 96.009mph
Valentino Rossi [Honda], 2003

2004 RESULTS
1st Valentino Rossi [Yamaha] 47m16.145s
2nd Max Biaggi [Honda] 47m16.570s
3rd Troy Bayliss [Ducati] 47m19.278s

2004 POLE POSITION
Makoto Tamada [Honda] 1m32.815s

GEAR NUMBER
1
2
3
5
6

50 mph
80 kmh

Turn 2

100 mph
160 kmh

Turn 6

135 mph
215 kmh

150 mph
240 kmh

60 mph
100 kmh

Turn 3

100 mph
160 kmh

Turn 7

Turn 11

120 mph
190 kmh

95 mph
150 kmh

Turn 10

60 mph
100 kmh

Turn 9

50 mph
80 kmh

65 mph
105 kmh

Turn 1

Turn 8

65 mph
105 kmh

Turn 4

Turn 5

85 mph
135 kmh

130 mph
210 kmh

65 mph
105 kmh

Turn 12

125 mph
200 kmh

Turn 13

75 mph
125 kmh

180 mph
290 kmh

65 mph
105 kmh

Turn 14

60 mph
100 kmh

Given that it packs so many corners into such a small area, the Ricardo Tormo circuit has a surprisingly high top speed, esecially as the adverse camber bend that ends the lap is so tricky. The fourth gear Turn 7 right up against the giant grandstand is not for the faint-hearted either

RIDER'S VIEW *Sete Gibernau*

"It's a strange little track – pretty much all corners, which make the tyres extra important because you're in and out of turns all the time. You have to make the whole lap work because there are no super-fast sections where you can make up half a second: you need to get every turn just right to gain a tenth here, a tenth there. The front tyre is really important because you need it to turn and grip while you're braking into all those tight little corners. Then straight away you're back on the gas, looking for as much traction as you can get to fire you out to the next corner, so the rear tyre is also really important. Like most places, it's the whole package that counts – you need a rideable engine, well-balanced suspension and plenty of grip and traction."

BIKES & RIDERS

Four Yamahas, seven Hondas, three Ducatis, two Suzukis, two Kawasakis, two WCMs, one Proton KR, and just one title

The section on each make of bike is followed by pages on each of the men riding that marque. You'll find a table for each rider showing their results in MotoGP. They are laid out with pairs of figures, like this: 1-2. The first figure is the qualifying position for the race and the second is the result. In this case, our man qualified on pole position but finished second in the race. If you've been watching bike racing for any length of time you probably know what the other abbeviations mean but for those new to the sport the panel below should explain all.

All the bikes are subject to 990cc maximum engine capacity. Honda use a V5, Yamaha and Kawasaki straight fours, Proton, Ducati and Suzuki V4s. WCM are starting the year with straight fours but promise a V6 soon!

ABBREVIATIONS

In the data panels on rider pages you will find a few abbreviations; here's what they mean:

f   Fell during the race
i   Injured, did not take part
dnf   Did not finish, usually as the result of a mechanical breakdown
dsq   Disqualified

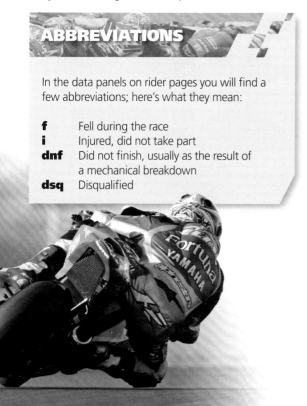

YZR-M1
YAMAHA

The 2005 Yamaha M1 incorporates all the lessons learnt winning last year's riders' and team titles. This year the factory wants the constructors' championship too

Valentino Rossi returns to defend his crown on the bike he transformed from also-ran to winner last year. The 2005 bike incorporates all the lessons Rossi and his crew, led by Jerry Burgess, learnt last season when there was a good deal of make-do-and-mend about the way the M1 was prepared. This year the bike is almost totally redesigned to incorporate the lessons of 2004. It's still an in-line four and the chassis still looks the same, but it's all new. The factory has tried to squeeze a bit more top-end power out of the motor but, at the same time, avoid losing the agility and precision which enabled Rossi to put the bike exactly where he wanted it last year.

One fact that should be borne in mind all season is that 2005 is the 50th anniversary of the Yamaha company being founded and, more than anything else, they want to win the constructors' title to celebrate.

Valentino Rossi and his vastly experienced Australian race engineer Jerry Burgess turned the M1 from also-ran to winner last season. Now they have to keep it winning in the face of a massive attack from Honda plus a resurgent Ducati and the fast-improving Suzuki and Kawasaki teams. It won't be easy.

It was the only prize they missed out on last year, with Rossi taking the riders' title and the Gauloises Yamaha squad snatching the team prize from Gibernau's Telefonica Honda team at the last race of the year. The constructors' title might seem like a very minor side issue to most of us, but the factories don't see it that way.

To achieve their aim – and let's be honest, it's Honda they have to beat – Yamaha will need some performances from their other riders. Last year, six poles, nine wins and three fastest laps were achieved on Yamahas, but the only one not set by Rossi was Checa's pole at Qatar. If you look at rostrum finishes, of the 14 times Yamaha was represented on the podium only three were not by Rossi – Checa's second in

France and Marco Melandri's consecutive thirds at Catalunya and the Netherlands.

In the championship Checa finished seventh, a massive 187 points behind Rossi. The other two Yamaha riders, Melandri and Norick Abe, were 12th and 13th respectively. Rossi only failed to be Yamaha's top scorer three times, when beaten into fourth in France and when he fell in Brazil and Qatar. In the light of those figures, it's very easy to see why Yamaha regard Colin Edwards as a good team-mate for Valentino. The American only failed to finish one race in 2004 – and that was when he was involved in the Motegi first-bend pile-up initiated by Capirossi – and he ended the season fifth overall, only eight points behind Barros. If you're chasing team and constructor titles Colin looks an almost perfect fit for your requirements. And of course, with a US GP back on the schedule, his nationality is a bonus.

Yamaha will probably have to rely on their factory squad for corporate points as the second Yamaha team is being used as a youth academy. The Tech 3 team's sponsor, Fortuna, had a big say in recruiting two young Spaniards, Xaus and Elias. Both are undoubtedly stellar talents, but they have just one year in the class between them: Xaus was the '04 Rookie of the Year but only 11th overall; Elias has great 125 and 250 form, but it's an early jump up to the top class for him.

The two Yamaha teams have vastly differing levels of experience. The Gauloises pairing of Rossi and Edwards has done 112 MotoGP/500 races, the Fortuna duo of Xaus and Elias just 16

YAMAHA
Gauloises

RIDER NUMBER **46**

VALENTINO ROSSI

Is this man the greatest motorcycle racer in the history of the sport? There are many who think so: enjoy him while you can

NATIONALITY Italian
DATE OF BIRTH 16 February 1979
TEAM Gauloises Yamaha
2004 SEASON Nine wins, five pole positions, three fastest laps (NED, POR, MAL)
MotoGP/500 HISTORY 80 races, 42 wins, 25 pole positions

What can you say about a rider who combines the natural talent of Schwantz with the technical abilities of Lawson or Rainey and the personality of Barry Sheene? F1 driver Jenson Button got it right on the BBC's 'Sports Review of the Year' when he said that Rossi is the dominant force in world motorsport. Not even the all-conquering Michael Schumacher can outshine him. There is no doubt that, while the new MotoGP four-stroke formula has helped rekindle wider interest in motorcycle racing, it's the talent and charisma of Valentino Rossi that has been key to the packed grandstands and increasing TV audiences. At every venue from Assen to Phillip Island there is a sea of yellow Rossi merchandise; every event is now a home race for the Doctor.

You have to resort to statistics to gauge just what the star has done in his relatively short career. There are, of course, the six world titles – 125, 250, the last 500cc and the first three (and so far only) MotoGP crowns. Then there are such landmark moments as the first-ever back-to-back wins on different makes of bike (Valencia '03 on Honda and Welkom '04 on Yamaha). But what marks Valentino out is his win rate. In percentage terms, Rossi has won 52.5 per cent of his 500cc/MotoGP races. Mick Doohan 'only' managed 39.4 per cent. Of Rossi's current competitors, only Max Biaggi is in double figures, with 11.8 per cent, and third best is Gibernau, with 7.25 per cent.

Last year he won the same number

Will this be his last year on bikes or will Valentino come back for more in 2006?

THE DOCTOR in MotoGP

2004 1st, Yamaha

RSA	SPA	FRA	ITA	CAT	NED	RIO	GER	GBR	CZE	POR	JPN	QAT	MAL	AUS	VAL
1-1	1-4	4-4	3-1	2-1	1-1	8-f	2-4	1-1	3-2	2-1	3-2	23-f	1-1	2-1	3-1

2003 1st, Honda

JPN	RSA	SPA	FRA	ITA	CAT	NED	GBR	GER	CZE	POR	RIO	PAC	MAL	AUS	VAL
1-1	2-2	5-1	1-2	1-1	1-2	3-3	4-3	4-2	1-1	3-1	1-1	3-2	1-1	1-1	1-1

2002 1st, Honda

JPN	RSA	SPA	FRA	ITA	CAT	NED	GBR	GER	CZE	POR	RIO	PAC	MAL	AUS	VAL
1-1	1-2	1-1	1-1	1-1	4-1	1-1	1-1	6-1	3-dnf	3-1	2-1	6-2	8-2	7-1	6-2

of races – nine – on the Yamaha M1 as he had done in 2003 on a Honda RC211V. This was the statistic that seemed to please Valentino most, as it proved the point he had left Honda to make, that the rider matters more than the machine. He also won more races and scored more points than any other Yamaha rider has done in a single season.

The big question hanging over this year is whether or not it will be his last in MotoGP, as his contract with Yamaha runs out at the end of the season. At the close of 2004 Rossi said that motivation would be more difficult to come by than in previous years, although he did drop a hint that he was thinking of staying for 2006. If he does it will be with Yamaha, as he admitted that going through the anguish of changing teams was something he had no wish to experience again.

Can anyone mount a sustained challenge in 2005 to Rossi's dominance, and if a challenger does emerge, how will he be dealt with? Valentino's usual act as the happy-go-lucky apprentice hippy has been dropped when more pressing matters have come up. Will it be the taunting he handed out to Biaggi, or the ruthlessness with which he undermined Sete Gibernau's confidence last year? If Makoto Tamada emerges as a contender, how will Valentino take care of business?

We should enjoy him while we can because, whatever happens, he won't be around motorcycle racing for much longer.

Rossi's achievements can only be measured against the records of the all-time greats. Only Mike Hailwood rivals him for the title of the greatest ever

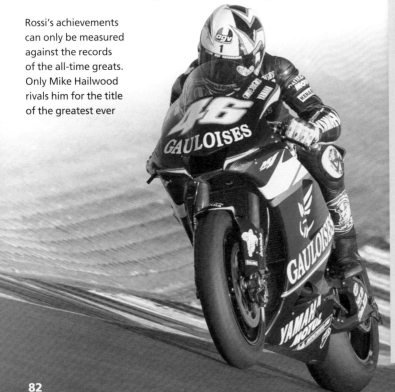

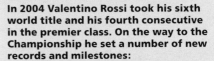

How ROSSI made history in 2004

In 2004 Valentino Rossi took his sixth world title and his fourth consecutive in the premier class. On the way to the Championship he set a number of new records and milestones:

■ At the opening race of 2004 in South Africa he became the first rider in the 55-year history of Grand Prix racing to take back-to-back victories in the premier class riding machines from two different manufacturers.

■ He also became the first rider in the premier class since Barry Sheene (1976, 77, 78 & 79) to win the opening race of the season for four years in succession.

■ The win in South Africa was also the first win for Yamaha in the premier class since Max Biaggi won in Malaysia in 2002.

■ The pole position scored by Rossi in South Africa was the first in the premier-class by a Yamaha rider since Max Biaggi started from pole at the last race of 2002 in Valencia.

■ The nine wins during 2004 were a new record for most wins in a season in the premier class by a Yamaha rider. The previous record was seven wins in a season held jointly by Eddie Lawson in 1986 and 1988, and by Wayne Rainey in 1990.

■ Rossi is the seventh rider to take four or more premier class World Championships. Giacomo Agostini has won the most with eight, followed by Mick Doohan with five and then Geoff Duke, Mike Hailwood, Eddie Lawson and John Surtees with four.

■ Of these riders only Giacomo Agostini, Mick Doohan and Mike Hailwood have previously won four consecutive premier class titles.

■ This is only the second time ever that a rider has won back-to-back premier-class titles on different machinery. The other rider to achieve this was Eddie Lawson, who won the title riding a Yamaha in 1988 and a Honda in 1989.

■ Rossi's title is the first in the premier class for Yamaha since Wayne Rainey won the last of his three world championships in 1992.

■ Rossi has now won the premier class title on three different types of machines in the last four years; V-four two-stroke Honda, V-five four-stroke Honda, straight-four four-stroke Yamaha.

■ In 2004 Rossi amassed a total of 304 points, the highest points total ever achieved in the premier class by a Yamaha rider.

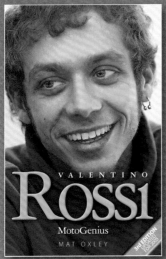
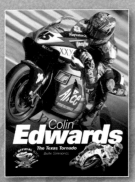

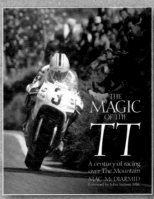
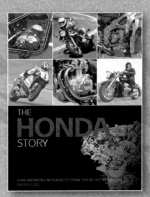

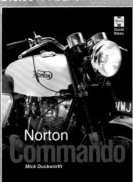
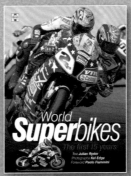
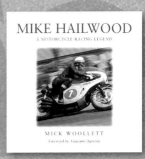

RIDER NUMBER **5**

COLIN EDWARDS

The Texas Tornado returns to Yamaha where his tarmac racing career started. Is the Yamaha M1 the bike he needs to win?

NATIONALITY American
DATE OF BIRTH 27 February 1971
TEAM Gauloises Yamaha
2004 SEASON Two rostrums, two fastest laps (GBR, QAT)
MotoGP HISTORY 32 races, 0 wins, 0 pole positions

The double ex-World Superbike Champion moves to Yamaha for 2005, making it three teams in his three-year MotoGP career. Most observers thought that he would be a sure-fire race winner last year on the Telefonica Honda, but he only managed two rostrums. However, his consistency netted him fifth place overall; the only time he didn't finish a race was when he became involved in the Motegi first-bend multiple pile-up.

The reason for his patchy performance? The curse that afflicted most of the Honda riders at one time or another last year: chatter. It affected Edwards more than the rest, and his cause wasn't helped by Honda only giving him the updated chassis designed to deal with the problem after all the other Michelin-equipped Honda riders. Strangely, he got it half way through the Qatar GP. Despite the Honda V5 being commonly regarded as the best motorcycle out there, Colin decided to switch to Yamaha and become Valentino Rossi's team-mate. What made that seem like a sensible thing to do?

There are, in fact, several reasons for the move. First, many of the Yamaha team personnel used to work with Colin ten years ago when he joined the Yamaha World Superbike team, then run out of Italy by Belgarda. The Texan speaks a good bit of Italian as a result of that period in his career and will be among friends. After the first test he said it felt like going home. You don't get that with HRC. Then there's the bike – the M1 has been developed around Rossi and seems to respond to a smooth riding style. Colin based his style on that of Eddie Lawson, the smoothest of the smooth, so no problems there. But what about having Rossi on the other side of the garage? They twice rode together in the Suzuka Eight Hour, winning in 2001, and show every sign of getting on well. Edwards also won the Eight Hour for Yamaha, with Noriyuki Haga, in 1996.

The idea of Colin going home to Yamaha is more than just making the facts fit a good story. Back in the States, his first tarmac racing was on a 250 Yamaha against the likes of Kenny Roberts Junior. Edwards was seen as the next champion off the American production line that had sent Roberts, Lawson, Rainey, Kocinski and another Roberts over to Europe to win world titles. The plan was for him to race in World Superbike, win there and then move smoothly onto 500 GPs. It didn't work out that way, though, and Colin had to go to Castrol Honda to win races and titles in World Superbike. There followed a spectacularly acrimonious fall-out with Honda over what he saw as their failure to make good the promise of a place in the factory MotoGP team, resulting in Colin taking the ride on the seriously flawed Aprilia in 2003 alongside old mate Haga. HRC most certainly did not enjoy the way negotiations were carried out in public on the Edwards web site, and conspiracy theorists pointed to this as a reason for what looked like his least-favoured status among last year's Honda riders.

Colin is one of a large number of MotoGP riders who won't see 30 again, and the only thing missing from his otherwise immaculate CV is a win in MotoGP. That's serious motivation.

Just like old times in Superbike: Colin chats with Ruben Xaus. They also met on the rostrum in Qatar last year

COLIN in MotoGP

2004 5th, Honda

RSA	SPA	FRA	ITA	CAT	NED	RIO	GER	GBR	CZE	POR	JPN	QAT	MAL	AUS	VAL
5-7	8-7	5-5	12-12	11-5	13-6	11-6	11-5	5-2	5-7	8-9	5-f	10-2	12-11	4-4	8-8

2003 13th, Aprilia

JPN	RSA	SPA	FRA	ITA	CAT	NED	GBR	GER	CZE	POR	RIO	PAC	MAL	AUS	VAL
9-6	8-f	11-14	19-10	13-9	7-dnf	9-7	9-10	13-14	12-12	13-14	12-13	13-17	13-13	18-16	7-8

YAMAHA
Fortuna Tech 3

RUBEN XAUS

He looks too tall for even a MotoGP bike, his style can look like a crash waiting to happen, but Ruben is always fast

Last season he brought his win-or-crash attitude to MotoGP and won Rookie of the Year. This year he's got a factory bike

NATIONALITY Spanish
DATE OF BIRTH 18 February 1978
TEAM Fortuna Yamaha
2004 SEASON 11th and Rookie of the Year
MotoGP HISTORY 16 races, 0 wins, 0 pole positions

RUBEN in MotoGP

2004 11th, Ducati

RSA	SPA	FRA	ITA	CAT	NED	RIO	GER	GBR	CZE	POR	JPN	QAT	MAL	AUS	VAL
16-dnf	12-f	15-14	14-5	7-6	9-7	16-12	18-11	10-11	10-f	18-dnf	18-9	7-3	15-13	12-11	17-f

Despite his years in World Superbike, Ruben Xaus started the 2004 MotoGP season virtually unknown in his own country. By the Catalunya round things had started to change. Xaus came to GPs with an unpromising ride on a year-old Ducati in the cash-strapped d'Antin team, yet he put in a stunning first half of the season. The disarray of the factory Ducati team helped him get noticed, but Ruben raced at the front of the six-lap Italian GP, and was then top Ducati at home in Barcelona and again next time out in Assen.

He didn't go quite so well after the summer break, until Qatar, a new circuit for everyone. Xaus was fast right from the first session and, as others fell or their machinery succumbed to the heat, he hung on in for third place and his first MotoGP rostrum. He tied up the Rookie of the Year title relatively easily but missed out on a top-ten position at season's end when he crashed at Valencia. And therein lies the enigma of Ruben Xaus. When he is good he is very, very good; when he is bad he crashes a lot. Without doubt he is blessed with great natural talent allied to bravery, which some opponents think borders on the reckless. He is also tall, handsome and fluently witty in half a dozen languages. In short, he fits the stereotypical image of a Spanish motorcycle racer.

The only question mark is over his ability to improve a motorcycle's set-up. His mid-season dip in form last year was seen as a function of this lack of experience. Ruben's profile at home will be raised immeasurably in 2005, but most observers expect much more than that simple objective to be achieved.

YAMAHA
Fortuna Tech 3

TONI ELIAS

He's won in 125s and 250s, now he comes to MotoGP as one of Spain's bright young hopes. You just know he'll be quick

NATIONALITY Spanish
DATE OF BIRTH 26 March 1983
TEAM Fortuna Yamaha
MotoGP HISTORY Rookie

It was inevitable that Toni Elias would race in MotoGP, the only question being whether he has come to the class a year too early. He is the first of the new generation of Spanish stars who have moved up through 125s and 250s to the top class, all of them looking to usurp those current rulers of Spain's motorcycling hierarchy, Sete Gibernau and Carlos Checa. Yamaha and their Spanish sponsor definitely had an eye on the future when they signed Toni.

Elias first came to GPs as one of a posse of talented youngsters discovered and nurtured by ex-racer Alberto Puig, in a programme sponsored by Telefonica and Honda. Toni stayed in 125 GPs for two years, finishing third overall in 2001, before accepting an offer from Aprilia to go to 250s. This move was not without rancour and was seen in some quarters as ingratitude at best and downright treachery at worst.

His three years in 250s yielded seven wins (to add to his two victories in 125s) plus overall finishing positions of fourth, third and fourth. Despite leaving the crazy teens behind in 125s, Toni took his win-or-crash attitude to 250s almost unmodified. He renewed his fairing-bashing acquaintance with Poggiali, with whom he used to fight on and off the bike in 125s, but it was an incident at Motegi last season that will echo for the next few years. Having diced with Pedrosa all race and ended up second, Toni announced that it was all down to Dani's light weight. As Pedrosa had come to GPs by the very same route

as Elias, but has stayed loyal to their mentor Puig and Honda, it was about the least diplomatic statement Toni could have made. Pedrosa won't be competing in MotoGP until next year at the earliest.

Enjoy Toni's bravado and the ever-present toothy grin, but keep a weather eye on the complex storm of politics that hovers over Spain's up-and-coming riders.

Toni has managed to adapt to the M1 much more quickly than most observers expected. He'll be a force this year

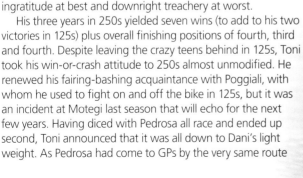

RC211V
HONDA

To beat Valentino Rossi the world's largest motorcycle manufacturer is sending out seven of the greatest racing motorcycles ever built

The RC211V is still, by common consent, the best motorcycle out there, yet last season Rossi and the underachieving Yamaha M1 won the title. Consequently, HRC (Honda's racing company) appear to have made more changes to team personnel than to their motorcycle. The most significant of these is the return of legendary tuning guru Erv Kanemoto to Honda colours as head honcho of the factory Repsol team, where he is reunited with Max Biaggi, whom he managed when the Italian won the 1998 250cc title. Both Max and team-mate Nicky Hayden will have new race engineers.

After the constant fretting last year about who was getting the best bits, HRC have made the position clear. Both Repsol riders and Sete Gibernau received works bikes at the start of pre-season testing. When new parts become available they will go first to the Repsol riders as they are the official factory squad. Expect Sete to get them about

Externally only the tail section is different, but HRC have found a few more horsepower and improved fuel economy. The invisible changes are to the engine management software and the motor's top end. The arrival of Erv Kanemoto is a much more visible declaration of intent

five minutes later, if he wants them (he didn't always last season). HRC also say they will wait to see a clear picture of the season emerge before they decide to focus their efforts on any one rider.

Too many people got hung up on this subject last year. It's worth noting

that the new engine HRC produced midway through the season, with two exhausts exiting through the seat, didn't win a race. Makoto Tamada's bike received no updates – and he was twice a victor.

This year, Tamada-san has his own team, the newly formed Japan Italy Racing squad, with sponsorship from Minolta and Konica. He also swaps from Bridgestone to Michelin tyres. The other two Honda teams are Fausto Gresini's Telefonica Honda, which again employs the runner-up of the previous two seasons, Sete Gibernau, plus Marco Melandri, newly recruited from Yamaha, and Camel Honda who replace Biaggi and Tamada with veteran Brazilian Alex Barros and Ducati reject Troy Bayliss. This year, all the Honda teams will run on Michelins.

New colours for MotoGP; new team and tyres for Makoto Tamada, Japan's great hope for the country's first MotoGP title.

Sito Pons's team is still yellow but the riders are different from last year's line-up

Only Sete Gibernau has seriously troubled Rossi over the past two seasons. He starts 2005 with a full factory bike and a lot of expectation on his shoulders

HONDA
Repsol

RIDER NUMBER **3**

MAX BIAGGI

The hero of all Rome and the bits of Italy that aren't painted yellow starts 2005 as Honda's number-one rider

NATIONALITY Italian
DATE OF BIRTH 26 June 1971
TEAM Repsol Honda
2004 SEASON One pole position, one win, three fastest laps (RSA, FRA, VAL)
MotoGP/500 HISTORY 110 races, 13 wins, 23 pole positions

At last the Roman Emperor gets what he's always wanted, a full factory Honda. Also, he is reunited with Erv Kanemoto, who takes over as Technical Director at Repsol Honda, having been Max's team manager back in 1993, when he first rode a 250 Honda. Max has been a World Champion for Honda: the last of his four consecutive 250 titles was won on an NSR250. And there in lies a clue to Biaggi's character. After a hat-trick with Aprilia he left the Italian firm and joined Honda to prove it was he, Massimiliano Biaggi, not the bike, that did the winning. Sure enough, after a season fraught with drama he won his fourth championship in a row – at the last race and by just just two points, but he had proved his point, at least to his own satisfaction. In fact Max made a habit of winning his titles at the last race, and against a variety of opponents. After one particularly brutal last lap move on famed tough guy Doriano Romboni at Hockenheim Max calmly opined that 'This is motorcycle racing, not the classical music.' No-one has a neutral opinion about Max Biaggi whether they've worked with him or raced against him.

Typically, when he moved up to the 500cc class in 1998 he won his maiden race at Suzuka. He was the first class rookie since Jarno Saarinen in 1973 to achieve that feat. In that first 500cc year Max finished second – to five-times champion Mick Doohan. Biaggi then moved to Yamaha, where he stayed until 2003.

He was Yamaha's lead rider when the MotoGP formula was introduced in 2002 and, despite the bike being seriously flawed, he won two races, making him the only person apart from Rossi to have won on the M1. His increasingly fractious relationship with both team and factory (where have you heard this before?) saw him jump ship to Sito Pons's private team and a Honda V5 in 2003. Again, he won two races; last year it was just the one.

Max has kept a comparatively low profile over the past couple of years, maybe because when he left Honda all those years ago the split was not exactly amicable. Whatever bad blood there has been in the past is now diplomatically forgotten as Honda search for the rider they need to beat Rossi, and Max for the bike he believes he needs to achieve the same objective. Many people thought that last season would have been his best chance of adding a blue-riband class title to his 250 crowns. It didn't work out that way, although for the first half of the year it looked as though it might. After his win in Germany Biaggi was second in the championship, just one point behind Rossi. He had a gearbox problem next time out, at Donington, which nearly put him out of the points, and then he became involved in consecutive first-lap crashes in Portugal and Japan which effectively ended his title hopes. He may have finished the season in third spot, well behind Rossi and Gibernau, but he can point to some seriously bad luck in the second half of the year.

It looks as if Max has every chance of challenging for the title again this season. At Aprilia he used considerable energy to ensure he was the only rider with a full works bike; now he unequivocally has the best machine Honda can field which, Rossi and Burgess notwithstanding, means the best bike on the grid. Biaggi always seems to have needed that type of validation of his status as the main man, so maybe it wasn't last year that offered him his best chance of the title: could 2005 be his season?

Max's super-smooth style should contrast nicely with his ex-dirt tracker team-mate's sideways style

MAX in MotoGP

2004 3rd, Honda

RSA	SPA	FRA	ITA	CAT	NED	RIO	GER	GBR	CZE	POR	JPN	QAT	MAL	AUS	VAL
3-2	4-2	3-3	6-3	4-8	12-4	2-2	1-1	8-12	8-3	4-f	4-f	24-6	7-2	7-7	2-2

2003 3nd, Honda

JPN	RSA	SPA	FRA	ITA	CAT	NED	GBR	GER	CZE	POR	RIO	PAC	MAL	AUS	VAL
2-2	3-3	3-2	5-5	4-3	9-14	2-2	1-1	1-f	3-5	2-2	4-4	1-1	4-3	6-17	6-4

2002 2nd, Yamaha

JPN	RSA	SPA	FRA	ITA	CAT	NED	GBR	GER	CZE	POR	RIO	PAC	MAL	AUS	VAL
5-f	4-9	7-exc	3-3	2-2	1-4	2-4	5-2	3-2	1-1	5-6	1-2	2-dnf	2-1	8-6	1-3

motogp

HONDA
Repsol

RIDER NUMBER **69**

NICKY HAYDEN

Nicky returns to the heavily revised factory Honda team looking for his first win. It took Doohan three years...

NATIONALITY American
DATE OF BIRTH 30 July 1981
TEAM Repsol Honda
2004 SEASON Two podiums
MotoGP HISTORY 31 races, 0 wins, 0 pole positions

Nicky Hayden enters his third year in MotoGP with the weight of expectation sitting heavily on his shoulders. The majority of the top class's heavy hitters are vastly experienced thirty-somethings; Nicky came to GPs in 2003 with no experience of racing outside the USA, having just become the youngest-ever American Superbike Champion. To add to the pressure, he was parachuted into the factory team of the world's biggest motorcycle manufacturer with Valentino Rossi as his team-mate. After a slow start he came out as Rookie of the Year, with rostrum finishes and some spectacular overtaking moves to his credit. By the end of the season he was universally regarded as the real deal.

What happened in 2004? To the worry of his team he again took a few races to get up to speed, and when he did get going he suffered a fall in Italy and then, that rarest of events, a malfunctioning factory Honda in Catalunya. Consecutive rostrums and then a fourth place at mid-season Donington suggested Hayden might be turning things around, but a crash in the Czech Republic while dicing with the leaders was followed by a disastrous training accident. That put him out of the Portuguese race and left him carrying a knee injury for the rest of the season. The knee was partly responsible for his crash in Valencia, the race which ended what looked like a season lacking in progress. In fact that is a harsh verdict, as can be seen if you scan Nicky's results panel: only Le Mans was an unmitigated disaster.

Honda has confidence in Nicky, and he has a new two-year contract to ride for the factory team. A little thought will tell you why. Check out the ages of all the top men, except Valentino Rossi. How many of them will be around in a couple of years? Indeed, it is not certain that Rossi himself will be in MotoGP beyond this season. Is there anyone else in their early twenties who looks to be in the same class as Hayden? Suzuki's John Hopkins is the only obvious contender. Ruben Xaus has a lot going for him too, but Marco Melandri has had a traumatic couple of years with Yamaha in MotoGP and ended last season totally out of sorts. Dani Pedrosa is the stand-out talent not yet in MotoGP, and there is also young Superbike ace Chris Vermeulen to consider.

Honda has already invested in Nicky, though. He won them that American Superbike title and then MotoGP Rookie of the Year. The next couple of seasons come under the heading of

'further investment', only perhaps with a little more pressure on the man himself. Hayden will have to hit the ground running at the start of 2005, but he showed last year that he knows how to learn – check out how his qualifying improved from '03. This year, he needs to rediscover how to win.

Teenage girls everywhere can keep buying those tickets; the Kentucky Kid is back and with a two-year contract in his pocket

NICKY in MotoGP

2004 8th, Honda

RSA	SPA	FRA	ITA	CAT	NED	RIO	GER	GBR	CZE	POR	JPN	QAT	MAL	AUS	VAL
4-5	7-5	7-11	2-f	3-dnf	16-5	3-3	9-3	6-4	7-f	i	9-f	4-5	6-4	14-6	5-f

2003 5th, Honda

JPN	RSA	SPA	FRA	ITA	CAT	NED	GBR	GER	CZE	POR	RIO	PAC	MAL	AUS	VAL
23-7	11-7	19-f	13-12	17-12	18-9	12-11	13-8	15-5	7-6	15-9	7-5	5-3	9-4	5-3	4-16(f)

RIDER NUMBER **15**

SETE GIBERNAU

Can the runner-up of 2003 and '04 find the strength of mind to fight Rossi on and off the track?

NATIONALITY Spanish
DATE OF BIRTH 15 December 1972
TEAM Telefonica Movistar Honda
2004 SEASON Five pole positions, including three consecutively; four wins; three fastest laps (SPA, ITA, CAT)
MotoGP/500 HISTORY 124 races, 9 wins, 7 pole positions

For the last two years Gibernau has been the only man able to trouble Valentino Rossi throughout the season, and he is one of the few riders who has beaten the champion in a head-to-head race, notably in Brno last year and especially at Sachsenring in 2003. So how come Sete is not in the full factory Repsol team, and does that mean he won't be getting equal equipment to Biaggi and Hayden? The answer is that Gibernau is contracted to Telefonica, not Honda, while Repsol's contract specifies that its colours will be carried by the full works team. In practice this means that Sete cannot have exactly the same stuff as the Repsol guys at exactly the same time. However, he will assuredly get it about a millisecond afterwards.

This issue of which Honda rider received what equipment bedevilled last season and seemed to distract more than one rider from the job in hand. The Italian and Spanish media seized on any rumour of a new part and blew the issue out of all proportion. It's worth remembering that the Hondas which did the winning last year did not come out of the Repsol pit garage, and that the new engine with the slash-cut rear pipes never won a race. Sete stuck with the equipment he knew and understood until he could do meaningful comparative tests.

He starts his third year with Fausto Gresini's Telefonica team surrounded by people he knows well and with the best bike in the paddock. It is a formidable combination. Gibernau is the very model of a modern motorcycle racer, as impressive off track as he is on it: dignified, well educated, multilingual and seemingly immune to the monstrous pressure of Spanish expectations. Some say he can be too emotional, and that he caves in as soon as Rossi starts the mind games. That ruthless master of psychological warfare, Wayne Rainey, was outspoken on the subject at the end of last season. However, Sete's bad races came directly after wins. He foundered in Motegi, unable to adapt to a new front tyre, and went missing in Malaysia.

This year he will have to eliminate such bad weekends from his game, because a bad result for Valentino Rossi is finishing fourth. At the start of the year Sete will doubtless also have to cope with all the politicking about equipment. Will Rossi renew the hostilities he opened after Qatar when he blamed Gibernau and Honda for his penalty? If he does it will tell you one thing – that the World Champion thinks Gibernau is a threat. The Doctor does not waste his time on people who are not serious rivals. Evidence? Long-time enemy Max Biaggi didn't draw any fire last year when he wasn't challenging for the title.

Sete has never done things the easy way, though. His only runaway wins have come in the wet, conditions under which he is clearly the best man. Other victories have been close fought or under the most extreme pressure: his first win came in the wake of 9/11, his most impressive after the death of his team-mate. He could very well find the strength to go one better this year than in the previous two.

In previous years Sete hasn't needed a works bike to beat Rossi, but this year he gets one. The man himself remains as dignified as ever

SETE in MotoGP

2004 2nd Honda

RSA	SPA	FRA	ITA	CAT	NED	RIO	GER	GBR	CZE	POR	JPN	QAT	MAL	AUS	VAL
2-3	2-1	1-1	1-2	1-2	3-2	4-f	4-f	2-3	1-1	3-4	13-6	3-1	4-7	1-2	4-4

2003 2nd, Honda

JPN	RSA	SPA	FRA	ITA	CAT	NED	GBR	GER	CZE	POR	RIO	PAC	MAL	AUS	VAL
6-4	1-1	6-f	7-1	6-7	4-3	7-1	2-2	5-1	2-2	4-4	3-2	4-4	7-2	3-4	2-2

2002 16th, Suzuki

JPN	RSA	SPA	FRA	ITA	CAT	NED	GBR	GER	CZE	POR	RIO	PAC	MAL	AUS	VAL
14-f	10-16	13-9	16-12	18-dnf	3-f	16-f	17-6	12-f	9-4	9-f	18-8	11-dnf	15-14	15-12	10-13

HONDA
Telefonica Movistar

MARCO MELANDRI

A Honda RCV and Italian management. Is this what Marco needs to showcase his talent in the sport's top class?

NATIONALITY Italian
DATE OF BIRTH 7 August 1982
TEAM Telefonica Movistar Honda
2004 SEASON 12TH
MotoGP HISTORY 28 races, 0 wins, 0 pole positions

Right from his debut in 125s Marco Melandri has raced with the weight of the Italian media's massive expectations on his shoulders. He replaced Valentino Rossi on the factory 250 Aprilia and emulated his friend by winning the 2002 title, although it took Marco three years rather than Valentino's customary two. His championship was won by a distance, so it's easy to forget that he was the youngest-ever 250cc World Champion. The previous season had perhaps been a better showcase for his talents, as he raced with, and from time to time beat, Harada and Kato. He also won his first-ever 250cc Grand Prix, at the Sachsenring.

Melandri also showed a willingness to come back from some injurious crashes amazingly quickly; he wasn't just fast, he was tough with it. He came to MotoGP as 250 champ, poached by Yamaha as an investment for the future when Nicky Hayden was spirited from their grasp by Honda. Marco went straight into the factory team, alongside Carlos Checa, but then suffered a broken leg in the first session at the first race of the year. The nearest he got to the rostrum was fifth at Motegi before suffering another injury, to a shoulder, when going well at Phillip Island. That one finished his season early.

To add insult to injury, he had to make way for Rossi in the works team for 2004, shunted sideways to the Tech 3 squad alongside Norick Abe. This turned out to be a marriage definitely not made in heaven. Early in the season Melandri suffered from arm pump and announced he would have to have curative surgery. Team manager Hervé Poncharal asked, through clenched teeth, why his rider had not had treatment over winter. Marco proceeded to put in back-to-back podium finishes either side of the operation, the youngest rider so far to stand on a MotoGP rostrum.

However, after his triumph at Assen, intra-team relationships and results went downhill. Melandri's best finish in the second half of the season was a fifth in Japan, and he didn't score a single point in the last four races. Team press releases were issued with 'no comment' where Marco's views on the day would normally have been printed. From Tech 3's point of view Melandri kept getting himself into good positions, then crashing – as in Portugal – or failing to get the bike working and crashing – as in Germany.

But Marco has youth on his side and Honda was happy for Fausto Gresini to recruit him to the Telefonica team to partner Sete Gibernau. The question for this year is whether or not the Italian can now translate the talent he showed in the smaller classes to MotoGP. There have been enough hints, especially at Assen last season, to let us believe he could be a force this year. And it's worth remembering that he will have to learn a new bike and a new team while continuing to shoulder the burden of the 'next Rossi' label that the Italian press has pinned on him.

If he can, for once, remain injury-free then Marco is quite capable of troubling the established stars of MotoGP

MARCO in MotoGP

2004 12th, Yamaha

RSA	SPA	FRA	ITA	CAT	NED	RIO	GER	GBR	CZE	POR	JPN	QAT	MAL	AUS	VAL
7-11	11-f	6-6	5-9	5-3	4-3	13-13	14-f	i	11-9	7-f	6-5	16-dnf	10-f	10-dnf	16-f

2003 15th, Yamaha

JPN	RSA	SPA	FRA	ITA	CAT	NED	GBR	GER	CZE	POR	RIO	PAC	MAL	AUS	VAL
i	i	16-17	4-15	12-11	14-13	8-dnf	3-f	12-f	17-10	11-7	16-11	9-5	14-11	7-f	i

HONDA
Camel

RIDER NUMBER **4**

ALEX BARROS

Now that Jeremy McWilliams is racing in the British Superbike Championship, Alex is MotoGP's oldest inhabitant

NATIONALITY Brazilian
DATE OF BIRTH 18 October 1970
TEAM Camel Honda
2004 SEASON Three third places, two fastest laps (GER, CZE)
MotoGP/500 HISTORY 210 races, 6 wins, 4 pole positions

After a year in the full factory Repsol team MotoGP's most experienced rider returns to his old chums at Sito Pons's Honda outfit. In 2002 Alex Barros was given a four-stroke for the last four races of the season: he promptly beat Rossi twice, then signed for Yamaha. It looked as if he'd be Yamaha's main man for '03, but after a great winter's testing the Brazilian collected a nasty knee injury at the first race of the year, which handicapped him considerably. Then, just as he was getting fit, he was torpedoed by Kagayama in practice for Donington and suffered a shoulder injury that blighted the second half of his year and was only fixed by some serious surgery in the off-season.

Honda remembered what Alex had done in 2002 and brought him back for 2004 to replace Valentino Rossi in the factory team. He started the year short of fitness but still managed third place at Jerez, where his lack of strength was not a handicap thanks to the terrible weather. The bad news came in the shape of two unforced crashes in Catalunya and Holland while he was looking good for a rostrum, at the very least, errors that were compounded by an identikit crash at Brno later in the season.

Being a works rider meant Alex had plenty of critics waiting to have a pop at him, and those crashes gave them plenty of ammunition. However, eleven finishes in the top six tell another story, and he had two really memorable rides. The pressure was really on him in Germany, where he was the only Honda rider supplied with a new engine, with the implicit suggestion that if he wished to keep his job he should up the pace more than a little. He produced a stunning charge from eighth after lap one to within half a second of winner Biaggi at the flag – and he did it on a set of ruined tyres that were visibly sliding at both ends and spinning wildly. In Portugal he reminded us that he has always been one of the latest of late brakers, holding off Gibernau in a dice for third that lasted most of the race. Alex never gave Sete a hint of a chance.

In the 2002 season Barros used the old 500cc two-stroke to harry Valentino Rossi at Assen. Rossi said afterwards it was the best he'd seen the two-stroke ridden that season. Further back in history he put an over-the-counter V-twin 500 on the rostrum at Donington, and he also has victories in the Suzuka Eight Hour endurance race on his CV.

Alex Barros is living proof that, in MotoGP, experience is one of the most useful attributes a rider can have, though it would be a mistake to label him as just a veteran. Last year he was widely seen as underachieving, yet he finished in fourth place overall, albeit well behind third-place man Biaggi. At 35 Alex cannot have a long career in front of him. But he wants to go out with a bang, not a whimper, so don't write him off – he won't be an also-ran.

Alex has been a Grand Prix motorcycle racer since 1986; he's raced every type of bike everywhere yet still is capable of racing with – and beating – the best

ALEX in MotoGP

2004 4th, Honda

RSA	SPA	FRA	ITA	CAT	NED	RIO	GER	GBR	CZE	POR	JPN	QAT	MAL	AUS	VAL
8-4	9-3	11-7	4-6	6-f	6-f	5-5	6-2	9-9	2-f	5-3	10-4	2-4	2-3	6-5	12-6

2003 9th, Yamaha

JPN	RSA	SPA	FRA	ITA	CAT	NED	GBR	GER	CZE	POR	RIO	PAC	MAL	AUS	VAL
8-8	10-5	15-5	2-3	9-f	5-8	6-8	12-i	11-f	9-7	12-11	11-12	8-6	12-15	16-dnf	8-6

2002 4th, Honda

JPN	RSA	SPA	FRA	ITA	CAT	NED	GBR	GER	CZE	POR	RIO	PAC	MAL	AUS	VAL
13-6	13-f	2-5	15-8	9-5	9-5	5-2	4-3	4-f	10-9	4-5	15-4	5-1	1-3	5-2	2-1

RIDER NUMBER **12**

TROY BAYLISS

When Ducati dispensed with his services Troy wasn't short of job offers. Camel Honda were the winners of that race

NATIONALITY Australian
DATE OF BIRTH 30 March 1969
TEAM Camel Honda
2004 SEASON 14th
MotoGP HISTORY 32 races, 0 wins, 0 pole positions

Troy Bayliss was a latecomer to motorcycle racing, never mind MotoGP. He didn't start competing until he was 23 but then progressed rapidly in domestic racing, along the way having impressive wild-card rides in the Australian rounds of World Superbike and 250 GP. His success saw him recruited to the British Superbike Championship by GSE Racing, for whom he won the title in 1999. He then went to the USA to ride for Ducati but was seconded to their World Superbike team when Carl Fogarty was injured. So for 2001 Troy headed the Italian factory's World Championship team and won the title.

When Ducati came to MotoGP in 2003 Bayliss was a natural choice to partner Loris Capirossi, as he proved by getting on the rostrum in his third GP. The first season was a triumph for Ducati and both its riders. Last year was anything

Can Troy adjust his all-action style to suit the Honda? You've got to believe it's a matter of when not if

but. The team scored just two rostrums all year, and they didn't come until the last two races. Development of the 2004 bike had taken a wrong turning, but Troy never stops trying. Unfortunately last year he tried a bit too hard a bit too often and crashed six times in racing. This did not go down well with the team, and you didn't need to bug the Ducati pit to hear the resulting discussions.

The season was such a disaster that someone had to go and it was Bayliss. The decision was announced before the Valencia race, at which he comprehensively beat his team-mate and got on the rostrum, as his replacement Carlos Checa crashed out. Troy dealt with the situation with great dignity, resisting the temptation to wave a finger or two in the direction of Bologna. Instead, he thanked Ducati, and the British and World Superbike Championships, for the good times. It wasn't an act – in private he said that he'd had some good years, and if he now had to suffer a bit then so what? That's the authentic Troy Bayliss, the family man with a proper sense of perspective. When asked which was the best day of his career he didn't mention the titles but replied that it was the day he no longer had to paint bits of metal for a living. The best demonstration of Troy's character came in the immediate aftermath of the first-turn crash at the 2003 Motegi race; Troy was one of the riders brought down and his bike wasn't fit to restart. What did he do? Stomp away in a fit of pique, wave his arms and demand the instigator be banned for life? No, he gave Colin Edwards a push start.

That side of Troy contrasts wonderfully with his racing persona. On Ducatis he was often visibly on the ragged edge, and his attitude to being passed by anyone was to bite right back at the next corner whether it was a good idea or not. Rossi realised this after a couple of spectacular dices early in 2003 and has adapted the tactic himself.

Ducati's loss was Sito Pons's gain, however, and for '05 Troy gets the bike that most of the paddock wants: a Honda on Michelins.

TROY in MotoGP

2004 14th, Ducati

RSA	SPA	FRA	ITA	CAT	NED	RIO	GER	GBR	CZE	POR	JPN	QAT	MAL	AUS	VAL
21-14	17-f	10-8	15-4	10-f	14-dnf	10-f	8-f	4-5	4-f	13-8	16-f	9-dnf	14-10	9-9	6-3

2003 6th, Ducati

JPN	RSA	SPA	FRA	ITA	CAT	NED	GBR	GER	CZE	POR	RIO	PAC	MAL	AUS	VAL
13-5	9-4	2-3	14-f	11-f	12-10	13-9	6-5	6-3	6-3	8-6	5-10	10-f	11-9	4-f	10-7

HONDA
Konica Minolta

RIDER NUMBER **6**

MAKOTO TAMADA

With a new team built around him, Tamada-san is many people's choice as the man most likely to worry Rossi in 2005

NATIONALITY Japanese
DATE OF BIRTH 4 November 1976
TEAM Konica Minolta Honda
2004 SEASON Two wins, three pole positions, two fastest laps (BRA, JPN)
MotoGP HISTORY 32 races, 2 wins, 3 pole positions

Is this man going to be the first Japanese champion in the top class of motorcycle racing? There are a lot of people who think so. Last year Makoto Tamada evolved from fast but inconsistent rookie to genuine challenger for race wins. Can he make the leap to championship contender this year?

Tamada certainly has the ammunition, a Honda V5 in a new team specifically set up for him, and Michelin tyres. Since he arrived in MotoGP two years ago he has been on Bridgestones. His two wins last season, at Rio and Motegi, came on tracks where Bridgestones seem to have an advantage over Michelins; but he also scored pole and a rostrum finish at Estoril where there is no perceived tyre advantage. The hope is that the tyre change will help Tamada avoid having weekends where he was totally off the radar, such as at Donington and Qatar. No Bridgestone runner has been able to shine in the wet, so we do not really know how he will go if it rains. Makoto also seems to have problems with Phillip Island.

Tamada came out of World Superbike and is only the second rider to win a World Superbike round and then go on to win a MotoGP race – the other is Mick Doohan. In 2002, when Colin Edwards and Troy Bayliss won every race bar one, it was Makoto who was the only other victor. Even back then it was obvious we were not dealing with the stereotypical Japanese loyal company servant. He does a lot of laughing and joking with his Italian team and sometimes outrages his Japanese translators with some very undiplomatic answers to journalists' questions.

There is, however, one subject about which he is very serious: the memory of his friend Daijiro Kato. After Kato's death, at the first race of 2003, Makoto checked the record books looking for races they'd both contested. He discovered that he had never beaten Dai-chan in races where they both finished. Tamada is utterly convinced that Kato would have been faster than Rossi, and therefore feels that if, or when, he wins the MotoGP title it will be proof that Daijiro Kato was the fastest racer there's ever been. It's easy for Europeans to dismiss this as sentimentality, but most Japanese will see the hand of number

MAKOTO in MotoGP

2004 6th, Honda

RSA	SPA	FRA	ITA	CAT	NED	RIO	GER	GBR	CZE	POR	JPN	QAT	MAL	AUS	VAL
12-8	5-dnf	8-9	7-dnf	9-dnf	8-12	7-1	13-6	15-14	17-4	1-2	1-1	13-10	5-5	5-8	1-5

2003 11th, Honda

JPN	RSA	SPA	FRA	ITA	CAT	NED	GBR	GER	CZE	POR	RIO	PAC	MAL	AUS	VAL
5-f	18-14	12-6	15-f	10-4	10-7	18-16	16-13	19-13	10-9	9-10	9-3	2-exc	3-10	17-10	13-10

74 guiding Makoto this year. Do not underestimate this source of strength.

Tamada has already shown that the Rossi mind games which have helped the Italian fight first Biaggi and then Gibernau don't seem to have an effect on him. Before Motegi last season Tamada announced that he would pay Rossi back for the way he'd tormented him at the previous race – allowing the gap between them to close, then pulling away. The Japanese was true to his word, taking pole and then winning the race from Rossi – and setting fastest lap on the way. He also set the fastest lap when he won in Brazil. Interestingly, Rossi's crash in Rio last season came just after Tamada had passed him. How the relationship between these two riders develops will be one of the season's more interesting sub-plots.

Get used to the colour scheme, you're going to be seeing a lot of it, mostly on the front of the grid and at the sharp end of races

DESMOSEDICI DUCATI

The switch to Bridgestone tyres is a high-risk strategy for Ducati Corse, but one the factory believes is worth taking in pursuit of race wins, if not the Championship

Modifications from the '04 bike are subtle but noticeable. New tail section is a work of art in its own right

Last year's most disappointing team are not going to make the same mistake twice. After a wonderful debut in 2003 they failed to test their '04 bike back to back with the race-winning original and paid the price, only making it to the rostrum in the last two races of the year. This year the watchword is evolution not revolution, with the only major change being the tyres.

In what is, at face value, a puzzling move Ducati have ditched the Michelins that won all but two races last year and taken up with Bridgestone. Why? The answer is simple: because they won two races. Ducati have tacitly accepted that, while Rossi is around, they can forget the title so the goal now becomes race wins. Judging by last year's results, Bridgestone riders had a significant advantage at

bike run by the d'Antin team for Italian 250cc refugee Roby Rolfo. The team will run Dunlop tyres, not the equipment of choice for anyone, but the boys from Birmingham are keen to point out that, with only the Roberts bike in their corner last year, they never had much in the way of track time. Dunlop's qualifying tyres have always been good – and there's nothing wrong with their rain tyres either. That matters because, when and if it rains, the outgunned privateer teams can hope to compete with the big boys as conditions negate power advantages.

The change to Bridgestone produced some teething troubles but Ducati Corse is now the lead team on the Japanese rubber

two tracks, Rio and Motegi. In 2004, Bridgestones set pole, won the race and put in fastest lap at both events. This was always a high-risk strategy, and now that Rio is off the calendar the prospect of a couple of race wins to keep an impatient sponsor happy doesn't look so certain. The change may mean that they will be at a distinct disadvantage at a couple of tracks at least, but that's a trade-off Ducati Corse and Marlboro have accepted.

To try and shorten the odds even further on a Ducati win this year, they are running a tyre test team using an '04 bike with the vastly experienced Shinichi Itoh as rider. He tested alongside the factory team pre-season and may appear as a wild-card entry at some races.

There will be one more Ducati on the grid for the whole season, a single

RIDER NUMBER **7**

CARLOS CHECA

There are people waiting to compare Carlos unfavourably with Spain's young chargers. Will they get the chance?

NATIONALITY Spanish
DATE OF BIRTH 15 October 1972
TEAM Marlboro Ducati
2004 SEASON One pole position, one rostrum
MotoGP/500 HISTORY 140 races, 2 wins, 3 pole positions

Before the start of last season Checa hadn't won a race for six years and hadn't even been on the rostrum for twelve months, a stark contrast to his form in 2002 when he came third in his first-ever MotoGP race at Suzuka. He didn't win a race in 2004 but he did set pole, in Qatar. He also got back on the rostrum at Le Mans, the only Yamaha rider to beat Rossi when both men finished the race. Carlos should actually have been on the podium twice, but the bike stopped on him in Qatar when he was a sure-fire third. His was hardly the worst performance by a works rider last season, but after three winless years Carlos and Yamaha have parted company. Some elements of the paddock regard this as a sponsor-led decision. It is undoubtedly true that a lot of Ducati's budget comes from Spain, and such is the popularity of bike racing there that Carlos generates an enormous amount of media coverage through the year, which is, after all, the reason for a sponsor spending its money. However, Checa also has long-term admirers in the upper echelons of Ducati management who were keen on employing him. Both John Hopkins and Shinya Nakano were candidates for the job, but Carlos's combination of assets got him the ride. The big unknown in this equation is the rubber, for Ducati switched to Bridgestone tyres over winter, a brand he has no experience of working with.

There may be mutterings about the Spaniard's record, but one thing is for certain – he's a tryer. In fact he is often accused of trying too hard, as in Brazil in 2002 where he charged past Rossi in the wet after being left on the line, only to crash a corner later, or at Donington in the same year when he crashed trying to fend off Valentino's challenge for the lead. When things go right, though, he is as fast as anybody. Stop/go circuits like Motegi and especially Le Mans seem to suit him, and he's always fast in Portugal. With three new

Carlos and the Desmosedici, another new partnership in MotoGP. How will they get on? Rather well, one suspects

circuits on the calendar this season the fact that Checa went well at last year's only new venue, Qatar, may be a pointer. As Bridgestone tyres seem to suit Motegi well, and Japan is a market where Ducati has invested heavily in recent years, the pressure will certainly be on both Carlos and team-mate Loris Capirossi to perform in the home of the big four Japanese manufacturers.

Not that any of this will affect Checa for, despite the unimaginable pressure the Spanish media heaps on him, the man always seems well balanced. He is a genuine motorcycle enthusiast and aware that, but for MotoGP, he would still be labouring on a Barcelona building site. Nevertheless, his performance will be scrutinised even more than in previous years. At age 32 Spain's old guard, Gibernau and Checa, have to look over their shoulders at youngsters Xaus and Elias in the second Yamaha team. The sublime Pedrosa surely won't be in 250s for long after this season either – and then there is the horde of talented kids on their way up from 125s. Being Spanish may help you get a job, but it won't ensure you keep it.

CARLOS in MotoGP

2004 7th, Yamaha

RSA	SPA	FRA	ITA	CAT	NED	RIO	GER	GBR	CZE	POR	JPN	QAT	MAL	AUS	VAL
14-10	3-6	2-2	11-f	12-4	2-9	12-10	7-f	7-6	6-6	10-5	11-7	1-dnf	9-9	13-10	9-14

2003 7th, Yamaha

JPN	RSA	SPA	FRA	ITA	CAT	NED	GBR	GER	CZE	POR	RIO	PAC	MAL	AUS	VAL
4-10	7-9	10-dnf	6-f	7-8	8-4	4-4	5-6	7-8	5-4	7-8	10-9	7-f	2-5	9-8	5-5

2002 5th, Yamaha

JPN	RSA	SPA	FRA	ITA	CAT	NED	GBR	GER	CZE	POR	RIO	PAC	MAL	AUS	VAL
4-3	7-5	5-dnf	2-f	3-4	7-3	6-3	2-f	10-4	6-5	1-2	5-f	4-5	5-7	20-11	5-f

RIDER NUMBER **65**

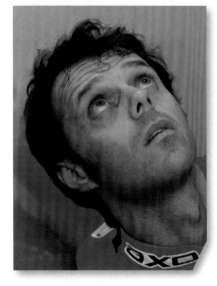

LORIS CAPIROSSI

Even Loris's fearsome will to win seemed to flag a little last year. This year expect him to make up for a bad 2004 season

NATIONALITY Italian
DATE OF BIRTH 4 April 1973
TEAM Marlboro Ducati
2004 SEASON One rostrum, one fastest lap (AUS)
MotoGP/500 HISTORY 105 races, 3 wins, 8 pole positions

In Ducati's first year in MotoGP Loris Capirossi was the only rider to beat the might of the Hondas, and he finished a stunning fourth overall. Catalunya 2003 was among the great races of recent years and also made Loris one of very few men to have won GPs on three makes of motorcycle (500cc Yamaha and Honda, MotoGP Ducati). On top of that he became the youngest-ever World Champion when he won the 1990 125cc title, then retained it the following year. He also became one of the most controversial 250cc champs when he torpedoed Tetsuya Harada at the last corner of the last race of the year in 1998. As Harada was Loris's team-mate, this upset quite a few people.

That dubious incident aside, Capirossi has always been the man you'd bet your life on to do one superhuman lap. In 2002 he put in some stunning performances on the outgunned two-stroke, notably at Motegi, and before the MotoGP era he was capable of taking quite astonishing risks over a whole lap in his quest for pole position.

The first season with Ducati was a continuation of that form, but last year was so disappointing that even Loris's legendary will to win seemed to flag at times. Everybody thought he would be a contender in 2004 not just for race wins but for the title itself – but he didn't get on the rostrum until the penultimate round of the season. There were flashes of the old aggression, mixed with frustration in Portugal and Japan when his rushes up the inside on the first lap caused all sorts of problems, first for Biaggi at Estoril and then for nearly everybody at Motegi.

No-one expects Ducati to repeat their mistakes of last year, but it's interesting to speculate on what effect the switch to Bridgestone tyres will have. They are sure to give the Ducatis (and the Suzukis and Kawasakis) an advantage at one or two circuits, but will they rule out a good result at other tracks?

If there is one rider you would put your mortgage on to beat the field in a single flying lap it is Loris Capirossi. He is willing to step closer to the edge for longer than most

Judging by previous years the answer has to be yes, at at least two venues. One thing is a racing certainty: Capirossi will add to his tally of pole positions. Bridgestone's qualifying tyres have always been good and no rider can exploit super-sticky rubber for that one banzai lap better than Loris. He may still be small enough to be on 125s, but he's someone even the tough guys think twice about picking a fight with.

The pressure will be on at Ducati this year. The factory is used to winning, and historically their fortunes in the real world of the showrooms have been directly linked to success or otherwise on the track. As a small factory, Ducati rely on their big sponsor to go racing and Marlboro is a brand that pays handsomely for success. The flipside of the coin is that they also demand it, so Capirossi will be expected to deliver. Whatever the demands, Loris will be his usual cheerful and combative self.

Loris and the Desmo ended last season on a high. Judging by the body language, he's still pretty happy with his bike

LORIS in MotoGP

2004 9th, Ducati

RSA	SPA	FRA	ITA	CAT	NED	RIO	GER	GBR	CZE	POR	JPN	QAT	MAL	AUS	VAL
9-6	15-12	9-10	8-8	15-10	15-8	6-4	10-f	3-7	9-5	11-7	7-f	6-dnf	11-6	3-3	13-9

2003 4th, Ducati

JPN	RSA	SPA	FRA	ITA	CAT	NED	GBR	GER	CZE	POR	RIO	PAC	MAL	AUS	VAL
15-3	4-dnf	1-f	3-f	2-2	2-1	1-6	7-4	3-4	4-dnf	1-3	2-6	6-8	6-6	2-2	3-3

2002 8th, Honda

JPN	RSA	SPA	FRA	ITA	CAT	NED	GBR	GER	CZE	POR	RIO	PAC	MAL	AUS	VAL
2-9	2-3	3-4	7-7	4-6	5-6	4-f	i	i	5-6	7-f	12-5	3-3	4-9	9-dnf	12-f

DUCATI
D'Antin

RIDER NUMBER **44**

ROBERTO ROLFO

Aprilia were gutted when they lost him; but things didn't go too well at Honda and now Roby is a MotoGP privateer

NATIONALITY Italian
DATE OF BIRTH 23 March 1980
TEAM D'Antin Ducati
MotoGP/500 HISTORY Rookie

Many good judges think Roby is a natural MotoGP rider. Will he be able to convince the doubters on Dunlops and an under-financed bike?

After 99 GPs in the 250 class, Rolfo moves up to MotoGP as the d'Antin team's sole rider. His bike will be a 2004-spec Ducati with the evolution parts with which works riders Capirossi and Bayliss ended last season. A couple of years ago Roby was a contender for the 250 title, but he never got to grips with the factory Honda that had been designed around Daijiro Kato, dropping from second in the championship in '03 to eighth last year. Previously he was an Aprilia employee, sharing a lot of the development work on the 250 GP bikes with veteran test rider Marcellino Lucchi. Rolfo also wore a groove round Mugello testing the 400cc V-twin that was raced against the 500cc V4s for a few seasons, and he's thought to have done some early laps with the RS3 MotoGP motor, although that hardly counts as proper four-stroke MotoGP experience.

Two years ago Roby was seen as one of the most promising young riders in the sport and was spoken of as a certainty for a factory team in MotoGP. He even got to test a Honda V5 at Valencia after the last race of the 2003 season. Now he's in MotoGP but as a privateer, on a steep learning curve with precious little in the way of back-up. Realistically, his best chance of achieving what Ruben Xaus did last year, getting on the rostrum for the d'Antin team, will come when it rains. Two of Rolfo's three 250cc GP victories came in monsoon conditions when he didn't just win, he ran away from the opposition. It won't be an easy year for Roby, but he will approach the problem with his usual intelligence; and then tell us about it in perfect English.

The New GSX-R1000

More power. More torque and acceleration. Less weight. Nimbler handling. Better aerodynamics. It's not a redesigned motorcycle. It's the reshaping of the entire Supersport class.

GSX-R1000

GSV-R
SUZUKI

A much improved bike, a world champion who's rediscovered his motivation, and one of the most promising talents on the grid: not a bad package

The Suzuki improved steadily last year, to the point where John Hopkins was happy to say that it was now capable of rostrum finishes

The only British-based team in MotoGP looks the same from the outside but, apart from their riders, nearly everything else has changed. Out goes manager of 28 years Garry Taylor and in comes Paul Denning, best known for running the official Suzuki team in the British Superbike Championship. In 2004 his Crescent Suzuki team took John Reynolds to the title.

Denning persuaded John Hopkins to re-sign at the end of last season, despite strong interest from Ducati, while ex-champ Roberts has a year of his contract left. Suzuki's bike made great strides last year, which was also their first with Bridgestone tyres. They got their 'big bang' motor half way through the year, but

the great advance really came in engine management, which had previously been erratic to say the least. Pre-season work during testing centred on improving that area still further. There is also a need to achieve a few more horsepower at the top end, to cure a top-speed deficiency. Doing this without reducing the bike's new-found usability will not be easy.

To help R&D, Suzuki are again running a test team. This year the rider is the vastly experienced Nobuatsu Aoki, who spent a season away from GPs developing Bridgestone tyres for their entry into the top class of racing. Hopefully Nobu will be making a few wild-card appearances this season.

New team manager Paul Denning, fresh from winning the British Superbike Championship in 2004 with John Reynolds

The old short, loud exhaust system hasn't been seen for a while the quieter pipes are more efficient. Neither of the riders is noted for his silence, though

RIDER NUMBER **10**

KENNY ROBERTS

Will an improved bike and new management rekindle the ex-champ's fire? Sure looks like it

NATIONALITY American
DATE OF BIRTH 25 July 1973
TEAM Suzuki
2004 SEASON 18th
MotoGP/500 HISTORY 129 races, 8 wins, 10 pole positions

The 2000 World Champion and scion of the legendary Roberts clan has the pressure on him this season, for he has a new team set-up, run by Paul Denning, an improved motorbike and a very fast young team-mate to deal with. It's been difficult to know what to make of Roberts over the last couple of seasons, and there are two distinct schools of thought. The first is that Kenny has quite sensibly refused to push his bike beyond its capabilities and risk injury for no appreciable return – or, as he would put it, 'bust my ass for tenth'. Popular perception has it that his team-mate John Hopkins had a much better 2004 season, but they only finished eight points apart in the championship, and in the eleven races for which they both qualified Kenny was quicker than John eight times.

You don't get to win a world title if you can't make a motorcycle do things it doesn't really want to. Most people are convinced that Kenny still has fight in him

The highlight of Roberts's season was a stunning pole position at Rio, which he followed with another front-row start next time out, in Germany. He was desperately unlucky to be the only man seriously hurt in the Motegi mass pile-up, and he tried to come back for the last race of the year at Valencia. Kenny rode one session and realised he couldn't go race distance, but he was the quickest man in that session. It was a classic piece of Roberts family theatre, and a reminder of how fast he can still be. He showed us the same sort of thing at Catalunya after pitting to change his rear tyre, coming out again to run at almost the pace of the leading duo of Rossi and Gibernau.

There is, of course, another view of his last couple of years, which is that Kenny has been going through the motions without putting the maximum effort into his work. His task this year is to persuade us all that this second view is outdated, plain wrong, or both.

It's worth remembering that Roberts won his world title on a bike that was most definitely not the best out there. He was both brave and crafty in his use of what was available, taking points where he couldn't win, playing the wet-weather regulations to the point where the rules had to be changed, and on occasion – as at Motegi – winning quite brilliantly. Intelligence and aggression were there in just the right mix. He timed it right too, for 2000 was Rossi's first year in the top class. The worst title defence in the history of GP racing followed...

The question for 2005 is how much there is of Kenny Roberts, World Champion, still out there. The most dangerous thing to do with Kenny (or any other Roberts) is to make assumptions about the way he will act under any given set of circumstances. This is the final year of his contract with Suzuki, so it will be fascinating to see how he approaches such issues as a heavily hyped team-mate and a (hopefully) improved bike, plus the challenge of the other three Americans on the grid.

It wasn't just Kenny's pole position in Brazil last year that impressed but the manner in which he took it – and the way he led the race in the early stages

KENNY in MotoGP

2004 18th, Suzuki

RSA	SPA	FRA	ITA	CAT	NED	RIO	GER	GBR	CZE	POR	JPN	QAT	MAL	AUS	VAL
10-dnf	10-8	13-12	9-dnf	16-17	7-16	1-7	3-8	12-17	15-10	9-14	8-f	i	i	i	i

2003 19th, Suzuki

JPN	RSA	SPA	FRA	ITA	CAT	NED	GBR	GER	CZE	POR	RIO	PAC	MAL	AUS	VAL
7-14	17-15	17-13	17-16	18-f	i	i	i	14-15	16-20	14-17	19-17	19-15	10-14	14-9	18-11

2002 9th, Suzuki

JPN	RSA	SPA	FRA	ITA	CAT	NED	GBR	GER	CZE	POR	RIO	PAC	MAL	AUS	VAL
10-f	6-dnf	9-8	9-5	10-f	8-7	3-6	8-14	i	19-11	12-4	16-3	8-6	12-8	12-9	14-dnf

SUZUKI
Factory Team

RIDER NUMBER **21**

JOHN HOPKINS

Only 21 years old at the start of the season and already a works rider for two years, a seriously fast kid

NATIONALITY American
DATE OF BIRTH 22 May 1983
TEAM Suzuki
2004 SEASON 16th
MotoGP/500 HISTORY 44 races, 0 wins, 0 pole positions

On paper it looks as if John Hopkins didn't have a very good season in 2004. That would be partially true: he had a terrible first half of the year followed by some massively impressive riding in the second half. Hopkins wasn't fit as the season started, thanks to an ankle-smashing supercross accident, and he showed no form until Donington Park, the ninth round. He suffered from other people's crashes too, in France and later in the season, at Motegi, as well as the Suzuki's

notable lack of power, especially before the revised motor arrived for Catalunya.

So bad were his first eight races that Hopkins was considered an odds-on candidate for the sack at the end of the year. He then put in a stunning ride at Donington, in a race where every other Bridgestone tyre user was totally uncompetitive, and scored a career-best sixth in Portugal. In that race he was over-riding a bike that was slow down the long straight and chattering badly as he forced it hard into corners to make up the time he'd just lost. Next time out, in Japan, he got his first front-row start in GPs only to be the principle victim of the first-turn multiple crash, collecting a broken rib and a deep – very deep – laceration to a buttock. Many pundits reckoned that, but for the crash, he would have been on the rostrum for the first time that day.

His luck was also out in other races in the second half of the year: there were a couple of blow-ups, and places where his tyres just didn't work – but paddock opinion about him turned through 180 degrees. At 21 years of age Hopkins was again considered a hot property. After all, as his then team manager Garry Taylor pointed out, if you're trying to beat a 26-year-old you don't employ a 30-year-old. 'Hopper' is one of the very few riders in the paddock who is both younger than Valentino Rossi and has substantial experience at the top level of GPs.

How John develops will be one of the most interesting aspects of this season. He came to GPs back in 2002 when he rode a two-stroke Yamaha against the first generation of four-stroke MotoGP bikes and scored four top-ten finishes. When WCM lost their sponsor they released Hopkins from

He was quick in Formula Xtreme, he was quick when he came to GPs on a 500, and he's very quick on a MotoGP bike

his contract and Suzuki snapped him up for the factory team. The first year of the MotoGP bike was fraught with difficulty, but in 2004 things did get better and John was able to say, quite honestly, that the combination of bike, tyres and rider was now good enough to put him on the rostrum. No-one argued.

Everyone's keen to see a new talent emerge, but British fans also like the fact that both John's parents were from West London and moved to the States shortly before he was born.

HOPPER in MotoGP

2004 16th, Suzuki

RSA	SPA	FRA	ITA	CAT	NED	RIO	GER	GBR	CZE	POR	JPN	QAT	MAL	AUS	VAL
11-13	13-15	16-f	i	8-dnf	10-14	17-15	12-9	16-8	21-dnf	6-6	2-f	11-8	8-dnf	17-15	7-12

2003 17th, Suzuki

JPN	RSA	SPA	FRA	ITA	CAT	NED	GBR	GER	CZE	POR	RIO	PAC	MAL	AUS	VAL
12-13	16-13	7-7	11-f	14-f	13-15	16-15	15-11	22-dnf	13-17	17-18	18-i	16-f	exc	13-12	17-13

2002 15th, Yamaha

JPN	RSA	SPA	FRA	ITA	CAT	NED	GBR	GER	CZE	POR	RIO	PAC	MAL	AUS	VAL
18-12	17-14	16-13	19-11	13-12	6-10	10-7	6-8	14-i	7-dnf	15-8	14-14	16-14	19-18	14-16	17-11

PROTON KR
TEAM
ROBERTS

Kenny Roberts continues his brave fight against the superpowers, this time with KTM power from Austria

The Kenny Roberts team's sponsorship by Malaysian car giant Proton may not be worth quite as much as in previous years, but they still have a very interesting bike on the grid this year. The Proton V5 motor has been replaced by a compact V4 developed by the Austrian firm KTM, best known for their offroad bikes. Originally KTM intended to run

their own MotoGP team, but the cost proved too much for a relatively small company. Their motor was already on the test bench when the project was shelved and, as the Roberts team had a beautiful cycle and no motor, joining forces made sense all round.

Tests at the end of last season proved the marriage was viable, but financial constraints mean the team will only be able to field one bike this year. The good news is that the Roberts team's association with a factory means they can get the tyres they want, in this case Michelins. True, finances will only allow for one rider but that man is 2003 British Superbike Champ Shane Byrne who was left stranded at the end of last season by Aprilia's decision to pull out of MotoGP.

With the bodywork on, the Roberts bike looks much like last year's, except with a slightly washed-out colour scheme and a strange exhaust pipe arrangement. Underneath is a totally new KTM V4 motor

The great news for Shakey fans is that the dreadful wrist injury he suffered in the Czech Republic last year has healed nicely and he starts the season fully fit

PROTON – KTM
Team Robers

RIDER NUMBER **67**

SHANE BYRNE

After a fraught first year in MotoGP, Shakey's back with a new team, new tyres and new bike

Shakey is thoroughy enjoying the Team Roberts experience. Before the season started he said how he felt like he'd already been with them for years. He's even coming to terms with working with one of his boyhood heroes in Kenny Roberts

NATIONALITY British
DATE OF BIRTH 10 December 1976
TEAM Team Roberts
MotoGP HISTORY 9 races, 0 wins, 0 pole positions

As the Aprilia factory has pulled out of MotoGP this year, Shane Byrne has moved across to Team Roberts. He was in competition for the ride with his old team-mate Jeremy McWilliams, but finally the younger man got the job.

Byrne came to GPs last year as reigning British Superbike Champion to wrestle with the recalcitrant Aprilia. Unfortunately it bit him very badly during practice for the Czech GP, breaking and dislocating his left wrist courtesy of a massive highside. Astoundingly, he managed to ride again in Japan before the severity of his injury was properly diagnosed. Before the Brno crash, 'Shakey' had qualified and raced at the same level as his very experienced team-mate McWilliams. If you look at the five races they both finished before the Czech GP, Shakey beat Jeremy three times. In the eight races they both qualified for in the same period, the advantage was split four each.

The high spots of the year were scoring a point in his first-ever MotoGP race, and then getting among the leaders in the six-lap sprint at Mugello while it was still wet. The low spots generally involved failing to get the Aprilia to do what he wanted during qualifying and suffering for it in the race. The worst of the worst came at Assen when the bike behaved

so badly that Shakey pulled in, something he has never been prone to. Now he has to help develop a new bike, a job most pundits agree would have better suited McWilliams. However, if the bike is anywhere near being raceworthy – and the signs are good – you can rest assured that Shakey Byrne will give it his best shot. It might even mean he can stop feeling so frustrated about being unable to show the MotoGP paddock how well he can ride.

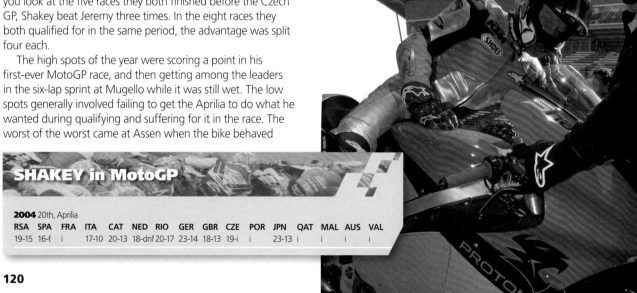

SHAKEY in MotoGP

	2004 20th, Aprilia														
RSA	SPA	FRA	ITA	CAT	NED	RIO	GER	GBR	CZE	POR	JPN	QAT	MAL	AUS	VAL
19-15	16-f	i		17-10	20-13	18-dnf	20-17	23-14	18-13	19-i	i	23-13	i	i	i

BLATA WCM

The team that have only just survived the past two seasons plan on having the only V6 on the grid by the third race of the year

The boldest engineering project on the grid is the work of the smallest team. Along with Czech minibike manufacturer Blata, WCM will field a couple of V6s. Sound unlikely? Well this is the team that took Niall Mckenzie to the 500cc GP rostrum as a privateer and masterminded Garry McCoy's wins. When the second and third races in the calendar were scheduled to be Rio and China, it was obvious that they would not take a totally unproven machine away from base in flight cases for three weeks, so expect to see the old straight four at least at the first two MotoGP events. The Blata factory wants to send one V6 to China but the team is not keen! Expect tests at Le Mans but maybe not a race outing. Getting on the grid will be a victory in itself.

WCM's racing manager Peter Clifford is confident that the V6 racers will be on track early in the season

The Blata V6 is not scheduled to embody any path-breaking technology; it'll be an across-the-frame engine layout with conventional valve operation and cycle parts. The noise should be good though!

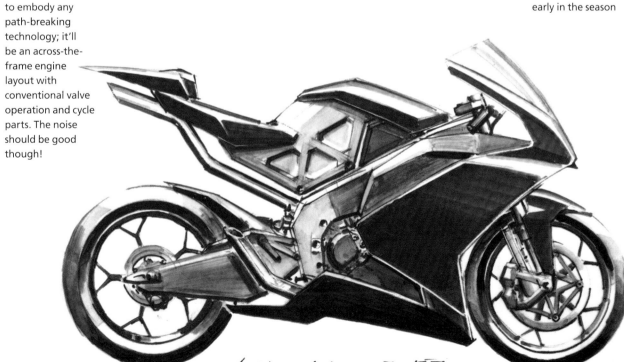

WCM
Blata WCM

JAMES ELLISON

The young Cumbrian has been there and done that as a four-stroke privateer, so he's back in MotoGP for a full season

NATIONALITY British
DATE OF BIRTH 19 September 1980
TEAM WCM
MotoGP/500 HISTORY 6 races, 0 wins, 0 pole positions

After impressing as a replacement last year, James signed a contract for 2005 at the penultimate race of the season. Ellison had a very busy time in 2004. As well as replacing Michel Fabrizio in MotoGP when the Italian fell out with the WCM team, he found time to compete in the World Superbike, British Superbike and World Endurance Championships. What's more, he scored points in all of them. In fact, that's understating his achievements. James won the privateer class of the British Championship and gave the Brit regulars in World Superbikes a good hiding when he rode the Brands Hatch round as a wild card on a Yamaha. In previous years he's been in Phase One's World Endurance Championship-winning team and taken two European Superstock titles.

All this adds up to the CV of a rider who, as a matter of policy, has gone out into paddocks where he might be spotted by factory scouts. Riding the uncompetitive WCM last year fitted the plan, and he rode it with enthusiasm and no little skill. Dicing with James Haydon (another stand-in, for Proton) for points and the honour of being top Brit in Qatar was the highlight of last year. The hope for this season is that when the Blata V6 arrives it will be fast enough to run with the slower works bikes, and reliable enough to be still there at the end of

a race when there could be a point or two up for grabs.

James Ellison takes the pure racer's view that he wants to compete with the best in the world and that means being in MotoGP. He has achieved just about everything that a privateer could in four-stroke racing, and as no works rides have come his way in lower status championships he feels there is nothing to be lost by taking another pure privateer ride in racing's top class.

James with the old four-cylinder bike during pre-season testing

ELLISON in MotoGP

2004 26th, WCM

RSA	SPA	FRA	ITA	CAT	NED	RIO	GER	GBR	CZE	POR	JPN	QAT	MAL	AUS	VAL
									24-f	21-16		22-13	23-18	23-22	23-19

WCM
Blata WCM

FRANCO BATTAINI

After a 250 GP career spent on Aprilias, Franco decided to try his luck with the smallest team in MotoGP

NATIONALITY Italian
DATE OF BIRTH 22 July 1972
TEAM WCM
MotoGP HISTORY Rookie

Franco followed the traditional Italian career path to GPs, starting 125 Sport Production in 1993 and progressing via the national championship and then one-make series. His clean sweep of the Suzuki Cup won him a place in Team Italia, the well-financed operation that took promising young riders to the European championships with good machinery, experienced mechanics and full technical support.

Franco spent 1995 and '96 splitting his time between the Italian and European 250cc championships, finishing third in both in 1996. From there it was on to GPs, and for the next eight seasons he was a leading privateer in the 250 class, always staying loyal to Aprilia. He started from pole four times but never won a GP, and was doing well in 2000 until a broken wrist at Catalunya ruined his season. Nevertheless, he was never out of the top ten from 1999 to 2004, with a highest placing of sixth in 2002 and again in '03. The 2002 result won him the Michel Métreaux trophy for best non-works rider.

It was Franco who approached WCM rather than the team making the first advance, but Racing Manager Peter Clifford had always been impressed with Battaini's willingness to get the most out of his bike, whatever its position in the hierarchy of 250 Aprilias. Crucially, from the team's point of view, Battaini comes to them with a wealth of experience at the top level, vital for developing a new bike through the season. Also, he is a very good wet-weather rider and that is the only circumstance in which the WCM, new V6 or old straight four, is likely to get among the slower factory bikes.

The first time Franco rode the bike he leaned it over so far he dug a footrest in and crashed; it ain't a 250!

NINJA ZX-RR
KAWASAKI

Kawasaki is the last factory to adopt a 'big-bang' firing order for their engine. It should stop them having those weekends where they struggled to be competitive

Without doubt the most improved bike of last season, the ZX-RR Ninja had a new chassis and tyres for 2004, and now it gets a new motor. Previously, Kawasaki stuck with the classic in-line four layout with even firing order. As a result, the noise that issues from it is the classic high-pitched wail we've known and loved for years. The other straight four, the Yamaha M1, ditched the even firing order last year and was transformed into a winner. Even the V4s of Ducati and Suzuki went for 'big bang' motors during the season. Inevitably, Kawasaki have gone down the same route. The theory is hazy but the results are clear: 'big bang' motors are easier to ride, give

tyres less of a hard time and win races.

Last year Shinya Nakano put the Kawasaki on the rostrum and on the front row – but also once found himself starting from the back of the grid. The new motor should hopefully even out that inconsistency. Like Suzuki, Kawasaki keep faith with both their riders and will be looking for that step up from occasional surprise package to regular rostrum contender. Like Suzuki, the team

Ichiro Yoda, recruited from Yamaha to be the Kawasaki team's technical director

Harald Eckl, manager of the Kawasaki Racing Team, and a useful (if lairy) 250 racer himself with a best GP finish of fifth back in 1984

Fiorenzo Fanali's CV is one of the most impressive in the paddock. His experience includes working with Eddie Lawson in the American's championship years

will now have to compete with the factory Ducati squad for the attentions of Bridgestone, their tyre supplier. No-one is talking about this as a problem, and indeed more fundamental problems seem to have engaged team manager Harald Eckl's attention over winter.

The perceived lack of know-how at Grand Prix level has been addressed by two stunning signings. First, Ichiro Yoda has taken the very non-Japanese step of leaving Yamaha, where he was in charge of the M1 project, and secondly the vastly experienced Fiorenzo Fanali has moved with Yoda-san to become Shinya Nakano's race engineer. Eckl describes Fanali as 'old school' and compares him with Jerry Burgess, Rossi's engineer, in experience and working methods. The old WCM engineer Christophe Bourguignon (known, inevitably, in the paddock as Beefy) stays as Alex Hofmann's engineer.

Kawasaki have spent a lot of money in MotoGP for, so far, one rostrum. The arrival of men like Yoda and Fanali shows that the factory understands what is needed to progress further. And let's face it, it's only Kawasaki people like Morita-san, President of the consumer side of the company, who would talk about the 'spiritual support' of their fans at Motegi for their 'Ninja warriors' on the track. It's so much cooler than thanking all your sponsors.

RIDER NUMBER **66**

ALEX HOFMANN

His first year as a full-time MotoGP rider was solidly impressive; now if he can just find a little more aggression...

NATIONALITY German
DATE OF BIRTH 25 May 1980
TEAM Kawasaki
2004 SEASON 15th
MotoGP/500 HISTORY 25 races, 0 wins, 0 pole positions

Germany's only MotoGP rider came to the class having been the Kawasaki team's test rider. Hofmann's wild-card rides for them in 2003 were impressive enough to get him into the race team last year. His tenth place in the wet at Assen in '03, when he comprehensively beat the two regular team men Andrew Pitt and Garry McCoy, even lapping the latter, was particularly noteworthy. He also scored points in his second race of that year, at Mugello.

So last year was Alex's first season as a full-time MotoGP rider – and as a German in a German team with new national TV coverage at home you could say he was under a bit of pressure. And that's before you consider that he had the excellent Shinya Nakano as his team-mate.

Predictably, Shinya was the faster of the two Kawasaki men; Alex never beat him in a race they both finished and only out-qualified him once. However, it was the gaps between the two riders that gave cause for concern within both the team and the German media. Team manager Harald Eckl tackled this problem in a novel way. He gave an interview to the top German-language motorsport paper in which he said that Alex wasn't prepared to stick his neck out when circumstances demanded it. Paddock gossip said that the paper was left for Hofmann to find just before first practice for the Malaysian GP: he read it, didn't say a word to anyone, went out and was faster than Nakano. What's more, this new-found aggression lasted right through the weekend. The rest of the team started worrying that Eckl would apply the same sort of incentive scheme to other areas.

In many ways the job of second rider is a thankless task. He gets everything second – Alex got to test the new 'big bang' engine after Shinya. He's not expected to beat the team's leading rider, but gets criticised anyway when he's beaten. Hofmann ended the season 32 points behind Nakano, but he did finish second in the Rookie of the Year standings, albeit 26 points behind winner Ruben Xaus. Alex may not have set the world alight but neither did he fail abjectly –

ALEX in MotoGP

2004 15th, Kawasaki

RSA	SPA	FRA	ITA	CAT	NED	RIO	GER	GBR	CZE	POR	JPN	QAT	MAL	AUS	VAL
13-f	14-13	19-dnf	13-14	14-11	11-13	14-11	16-10	21-19	26-13	17-13	19-10	18-9	13-dnf	8-13	11-11

2003 23rd, Kawasaki

JPN	RSA	SPA	FRA	ITA	CAT	NED	GBR	GER	CZE	POR	RIO	PAC	MAL	AUS	VAL
	21-16		15-14		17-10			21-17	20-19						

2002 22nd, Yamaha & Honda

JPN	RSA	SPA	FRA	ITA	CAT	NED	GBR	GER	CZE	POR	RIO	PAC	MAL	AUS	VAL
					19-dnf	12-11	19-17	19-10							

Kawasaki have experimented with several exhaust systems, but this twin-pipe version does seem a bit retro

indeed, he finished above both Suzukis, Neil Hodgson and the Aprilias. He dealt with the Kawasaki's frequent engine blow-ups philosophically for the most part and was capable of fighting back from a bad start, as at Valencia where he caught and passed Jeremy McWilliams and John Hopkins, neither of whom are soft touches.

However, there is undoubtedly some basis to Harald Eckl's criticisms; the team manager will want to see more finishes inside the top ten than the two Alex managed last year. There's also the matter of a ride in 2006, because this is the final year of his contract with the Kawasaki team. Last season was Alex's first full year in MotoGP, though, so there's every chance in 2005 of the improvement his team want to see.

Alex remains Germany's only rider in MotoGP and, in the absence of any young guns, the only high-profile German racer

KAWASAKI
Factory Team

RIDER NUMBER **56**

SHINYA NAKANO

Super Shinya is one of the safest, smoothest riders around. He only had one crash last year; but it was the fastest ever

NATIONALITY Japanese
DATE OF BIRTH 10 October 1977
TEAM Kawasaki
2004 SEASON One rostrum
MotoGP/500 HISTORY 63 races, 0 wins, 0 pole positions

Despite an approach from Ducati, Shinya Nakano is staying with Kawasaki for 2005, having given them their first rostrum of the MotoGP era at Motegi last year. Twelve months ago his ambition was to finish the year in the top ten; he did it. This year his objectives are to finish in the top six of the championship and score a few more rostrums. Ambitious? Certainly. Impossible? Absolutely not.

Nakano gets Kawasaki's new 'big bang' motor, which should make the bike much more manageable, and the recruitment of ex-M1 project leader Yoda-san from Yamaha will give the team much-needed Grand Prix experience. Shinya will also have Fiorenzo Fanali as his chief mechanic. The Italian's experience goes back to MV Agusta, but in recent times he's been a Yamaha man. Last year the usually unflappable Nakano occasionally became exasperated with his Japanese bosses when they failed to take notice of his views. The two new key team members should help to solve that problem.

Last season was Shinya's first away from Yamaha, for whom he'd been a works rider since 1997. The following year he won the Japanese 250cc championship before going to GPs, where he had six 250 victories and only lost the 2000 world title to his team-mate, Olivier Jacque, on the last lap of the final race of the season. Then it was up to 500s where he scored his only rostrum until last year, at the Sachsenring, in 2001. After that Nakano seemed to lose the confidence of the factory and, to most people's surprise, had to cede the last Yamaha seat for '04 to Norick Abe.

Shinya went to Kawasaki, who'd had a terrible first year in MotoGP. But a new chassis and new tyres made the ZX-RR Ninja the most improved bike of last season and Nakano put in some inspired rides in qualifying as well as races – five second-row starts and four top-ten finishes before getting on the front row in Malaysia and the rostrum in Japan. Amazingly, he only had one crash all year, including private testing – but what a crash. His rear tyre let go at a terrifying 200mph on the front straight at Mugello; despite bouncing and sliding for what seemed like forever, he escaped serious injury. A week later he finished seventh at Barcelona, taking Biaggi on the last corner.

The contrast between this sort of behaviour and the charming, youthful Shinya is quite astounding. He retains the innate courtesy of the Japanese, but four years living in France followed by two in Barcelona mean he also has the European tendency to tell it like it is.

He is universally liked in the paddock and a lot of very good riders will tell you what a fine racer he is. His smooth, almost classical style is much admired. Thanks to his years with the Tech 3 team Shinya is especially popular in France, where he is regarded as an honorary citizen by the fans – look out for banners supporting him at Le Mans.

Nakano characterises the German Eckl outfit that runs Kawasaki's MotoGP team as being very Japanese in the way it works, strict and with no illusions. If they can keep up the momentum generated last year, Shinya's ambitions may again be realised.

Shinya's third place at Motegi last year was the most popular rostrum finish of the season. A repeat performance would be a great achievement

SHINYA in MotoGP

2004 10th, Kawasaki														
RSA	SPA	FRA	ITA	CAT	NED	RIO	GER	GBR	CZE	POR	JPN	QAT	MAL	AUS	VAL
6-12	6-9	12-dnf	10-f	13-7	5-dnf	9-9	5-7	11-15	23-12	12-11	12-3	5-dnf	3-8	11-12	10-7

2003 10th, Yamaha														
JPN	RSA	SPA	FRA	ITA	CAT	NED	GBR	GER	CZE	POR	RIO	PAC	MAL	AUS	VAL
10-9	5-11	13-8	9-14	3-5	6-5	10-13	11-9	10-7	14-14	6-12	6-8	12-9	5-8	11-7	12-f

2002 11th, Yamaha														
JPN	RSA	SPA	FRA	ITA	CAT	NED	GBR	GER	CZE	POR	RIO	PAC	MAL	AUS	VAL
9-dnf	8-8	14-17	10-13	14-11	10-f	14-8	15-10	2-5	11-dnf	17-12	13-dnf	17-16	16-6	16-13	9-6

THE SUPPORT CLASSES
125s & 250s

Can Chaz Davies and his low-budget team again impress against the well-funded factory teams? Will the new influx of young talent to the 125 class unearth a new Pedrosa?

With due respect to Shakey and James Ellison, the UK's best chance of Grand Prix glory this year lies with Chaz Davies. The Hertfordshire teenager ended last year with a brace of top-six finishes to underline just what a talent he is. For 2005, his third year in the 250cc class, he stays with the Aprilia Germany team but with some slightly newer equipment. An '03 chassis replaces the 1998 model (really!) he used last year and he has been told he will have some uprated cylinders. The bad news is that he is up against six factory Aprilias (Stoner,

Locatelli, Corsi, de Angelis, Porto and de Puniet) and a similar number of top-spec Hondas led by defending world champion Dani Pedrosa.

Getting in the top ten will be a major achievement and Chaz knows it. He says that fast flowing circuits are the places he can expect to do well, the places where carrying corner speed is the key, not outright power. Nevertheless, it's worth noting his best finish of last year came on the tight and twisty Valencia track; the boy is good.

His main target for the year is the IRTA

British fans' hopes in the support classes lie with Chaz Davies, the teenager from the borders, and his Aprilia Germany team

125cc CLASS

No.	Rider	Nat	Machine	Team
6	Joan Olive	SPA	Aprilia	Nocable.it Race
7	Alexis Masbou	FRA	Honda	Ajo Motosport
8	Lorenzo Zanetti	ITA	Aprilia	Fontana Racing
9	Toshihisa Kuzuhara	JPN	Honda	Angaia Racing
10	Federico Sandi	ITA	Honda	Angaia Racing
11	Sandro Cortese	GER	Honda	Kiefer - Bos - Castrol Honda
12	Thomas Lüthi	SUI	Honda	Elit Grand Prix
14	Gabor Talmacsi	HUN	KTM	Red Bull KTM GP125
15	Michele Pirro	ITA	Malaguti	Malaguti Reparto Corse
16	Raymond Schouten	NED	Honda	Arie Molenaar Racing
18	Nicolas Terol	SPA	Derbi	Caja Madrid - Derbi Racing
19	Alvaro Bautista	SPA	Honda	Seedorf RC3 - Club Tiempo Holidays
22	Pablo Nieto	SPA	Derbi	Caja Madrid - Derbi Racing
25	Dario Giuseppetti	GER	Aprilia	AB Cardion Blauer USA
26	Vincent Braillard	SUI	Aprilia	Road Racing Team Hungary
28	Jordi Carchano	SPA	Aprilia	MVA Aspar Team
29	Andrea Iannone	ITA	Aprilia	Abruzzo Racing Team
31	Sascha Hommel	GER	Malaguti	Malaguti Reparto Corse
32	Fabrizio Lai	ITA	Honda	Racing World
33	Sergio Gadea	SPA	Aprilia	Master Aspar Team
35	Raffael de Rosa	ITA	Aprilia	Matteoni Racing
36	Mika Kallio	FIN	KTM	Red Bull KTM GP125
41	Alex Espargaro	SPA	Honda	Seedorf RC3 - Club Tiempo Holidays
43	Manuel Hernandez	SPA	Aprilia	Totti Top Sport - 3C
44	Karel Abraham	CZE	Aprilia	AB Cardion Blauer USA
45	Imre Toth	HUN	Aprilia	Road Racing Team Hungary
47	Angel Rodriguez	SPA	Honda	Galicia Team
52	Lukas Pesek	CZE	Derbi	Metis Racing Team
54	Manuel Poggiali	RSM	Gilera	Metis Racing Team
55	Hector Faubel	SPA	Aprilia	Master Aspar Team
58	Marco Simoncelli	ITA	Aprilia	Nocable-it Race
60	Julian Simon	SPA	KTM	Red Bull KTM GP125
63	Mike di Meglio	FRA	Honda	Racing World
71	Tomoyoshi Koyama	JPN	Honda	Ajo Motosport
75	Mattia Pasini	ITA	Aprilia	Totti Top Sport - 3C
84	Julian Miralles	SPA	Aprilia	MVA Aspar Team

250cc CLASS

No.	Rider	Nat	Machine	Team
1	Daniel Pedrosa	SPA	Honda	Telefonica Movistar Honda 250cc
5	Alex de Angelis	RSM	Aprilia	MS Aprilia Italia Corse
6	Alex Debon	SPA	Honda	Wurth Honda BQR
7	Randy de Puniet	FRA	Aprilia	Aprilia Aspar Team 250cc
8	Andrea Ballerini	ITA	Aprilia	Abruzzo Racing Team
9	Hugo Marchand	FRA	Yamaha	Team UGT Kurz
12	Frederik Watz	SWE	Yamaha	Team UGT Kurz
14	Anthony West	AUS	KTM	Red Bull KTM GP250
15	Roberto Locatelli	ITA	Aprilia	Carrera Sunglasses - LCR
17	Steve Jenkner	GER	Aprilia	Nocable.it Race
19	Sebastian Porto	ARG	Aprilia	Aprilia Aspar Team 250cc
20	Gabriele Ferro	ITA	Fantic	Scuderia Fantic Motor GP
21	Arnaud Vincent	FRA	Fantic	Scuderia Fantic Motor GP
24	Simone Corsi	ITA	Aprilia	MS Aprilia Italia Corse
25	Alex Baldolini	ITA	Aprilia	Campetella Racing
27	Casey Stoner	AUS	Aprilia	Carrera Sunglasses - LCR
28	Dirk Heidolf	GER	Honda	Kiefer - Bos - Castrol Honda
32	Mirko Giansanti	ITA	Aprilia	Matteoni Racing
34	Andrea Dovizioso	ITA	Honda	Team Scot
36	Martin Cardenas	COL	Aprilia	Aprilia Team Germany
38	Gregory Leblanc	FRA	Aprilia	Equipe GP de France - Scrab
44	Taro Sekiguchi	JPN	Aprilia	Campetella Racing
48	Jorge Lorenzo	SPA	Honda	Fortuna Lotus Honda
50	Sylvain Guintoli	FRA	Aprilia	Equipe GP de France - Scrab
55	Yuki Takahashi	JPN	Honda	Team Scot
57	Chaz Davies	GBR	Aprilia	Aprilia Germany
64	Radomil Rous	CZE	Honda	Wurth Honda BQR
73	Hiroshi Aoyama	JPN	Honda	Telefonica Movistar Honda 250cc
80	Hector Barbera	SPA	Honda	Fortuna Lotus Honda
96	Jakub Smrz	CZE	Honda	Arie Molenaar Racing

Last year Dani Pedrosa won his first 250 GP and became world champion in his rookie year: a stellar talent

Cup for non-factory riders. He sees Debon, Giansanti and maybe Steve Jenkner as the opposition for that title, and any finish outside the points will be regarded as a failure.

Scoring big points in the 250 class will be more difficult than last year as a new age limit of 28 years old comes into force in the 125s. That has forced a migration of some very experienced riders, like Locatelli and Jenkner, to the 250s. And they have been accompanied by a gaggle of the crazy teenagers that so enlivened the 125 class last year, provided you were watching from the safety of the stands. Reigning 125 champion Andrea Dovizioso impressed mightily pre-season.

This has left the 125s in a state of flux. There are a host of new candidates for race wins and rostrum positions. It will be interesting to see how KTM fare with three factory bikes. Their 250 for top privateer of 2004 Ant West should be on track for the Le Mans GP.

The 125 favourites should be Pablo Nieto and Alvaro Bautista, but the joker in the pack is ex-champion Manuel Poggiali, back in the 125s after a disastrous defence of his 250 crown. If he can get his head together anything could happen.

RIDERS FOR HEALTH
RIGHT ON TRACK FOR AFRICA

Riders for Health is the pioneering organisation that runs cost-effective motorcycle management systems in Africa to ensure that thousands of lives are saved and transformed throughout the continent. And it all started in the GP paddock...

If you are trying to bring health care to remote communities a motorcycle is the obvious mode of transport

Sometimes, you wonder if it was a good idea. It's midnight ... Donington Park ... Day of Champions. We stand exhausted in the paddock after a marathon slog, and wonder why the hell we do it. Every year it's a huge hassle, a huge stress.

Well, we do it because we know what real stress is. It's losing your wife during childbirth because the ambulance that was taking her to hospital broke down. It's seeing the wretched shivering of malaria run through your children because no-one could get to your village to deliver mosquito nets. It's living with the pain of AIDS and feeling like a burden on your family because you can't

Day of Champions on the Thursday before the Donington GP is the main UK fundraiser for RfH. Everybody goes

reach the clinic to get the drugs you need.

Public health care given by trained health workers is the key to improving health and life chances in Africa, but an African public health worker has a hard target to reach – delivering health care to 20,000 women, men and children living in small communities scattered across the barren, inhospitable landscape of rural Africa. For these people to have a chance of survival, it is vital that their assigned health worker succeeds in reaching them, day in day out. She/he is the lifeline for some of the world's poorest, most disadvantaged people who have no other means of accessing

help in the fight against easily treatable and preventable disease.

There is no traditional transport infrastructure in Africa. Public transport is limited and, in the rural areas with the highest density of population, the biggest roads are little more than cart tracks. Most villages are accessible only after crossing boulder-strewn, dust-shrouded scrubland. So what is the ideal vehicle for reaching these remote villages? The motorcycle.

Look in Mr Blair's Africa Commission report, and you'll learn that 'Many health workers do not have transport to reach patients.' Look in the footnote and you'll see that Riders for Health told

them that. We noticed the problem back in 1988, in Somalia, when a British nurse told us, 'We can't reach these people here. They're nomads. We don't have any transport.' At the back of the hospital compound stood an almost-new $30,000 Land Cruiser, grounded forever for the want of a three-dollar part. Not exactly rocket science, is it? So for the last 15 years we've been working – very successfully – to turn this situation around. Now our innovative, sustainable transport management systems ensure that health workers have vehicles that never break down and are run at the lowest possible cost.

This year Riders aims to mobilise even more rural communities in Africa. Our unique partnership with MotoGP is saving lives, and your support really does matter and help us to achieve our goals.

Riders' current projects in need of funding focus on:

- improving outreach maintenance facilities for the growing number of health delivery vehicles, so that health care can be delivered to communities reliably and predictably;
- training even more health workers to ride and drive safely so that they can reach their communities;
- establishing community-based transport for hospital referrals and emergency situations.

The fundraising events taking place in the paddock this year will make a huge difference to these programmes.

Last year MotoGP helped Riders for Health to raise almost a quarter of a million pounds, and we truly value the support that has been given within the paddock. With your help we are taking thousands and thousands of people out of the suffering caused by ill-health, giving them the strength to fight poverty. Our ultimate goal is to ensure that reliable transportation is available for the delivery of health care across Africa by 2015, and all the money you raise will help us to reach this target!

Andrea Coleman

RULES & REGULATIONS

They're all detailed here, including new-for-2005 features such as the definition of a change from a 'dry' to a 'wet' race

BEFORE THE START

Pit lane opens 20 minutes (15 minutes for the 125 and 250 races) before the start. Riders can do a lap and stop on the grid or pass through pit lane to do more than one lap before stopping. The rider can stop at his pit for work on his bike, to top up the petrol tank, or even to swap bikes.

Pit lane closes 15 minutes (ten minutes for the smaller classes) before the start. Riders still in pit lane may start the warm-up lap from the pit lane exit but must start the race from the back of the grid. This can be a useful tactic in changeable weather conditions or if a major set-up problem comes to light.

However, those riders in pit lane cannot change wheels once the three-minute board has been shown.

The warm-up lap is started with two minutes to go before the start.

THE START

Bikes must be stationary with their front wheels up to the white line that defines the grid. From this year, the grid for MotoGP will be in rows of three, not four.

The race is started by lights. Red lights go on and stay on for two to five seconds: when they go out the race starts. Bikes must not move while the red lights are on.

If a rider has a problem on the grid the start may be delayed. Yellow lights will flash and a Start Delayed board will be shown. There will be another warm-up lap and the race distance will be shortened by a lap.

WET OR DRY

MotoGP races will no longer be interrupted for climatic reasons.

There are no changes to the 125 and 250 race regulations. If a race is stopped the result is annulled and used to decide grid positions for a second start. This second race will decide the result without reference to the annulled race. Race distance will be the number of laps left when the non-race was stopped, but will never be less than five laps. Only riders who finished the first race will be allowed to restart.

All races will be categorised as either wet or dry. A board may be displayed on the grid to indicate the status of the race. If no board is displayed, the race is automatically dry. The purpose of this classification is to indicate to riders the consequence of varying climatic conditions during a race.

Race Direction decides which of these terms apply before the start – and it doesn't always depend on the weather.

A 'Dry' race will be stopped and restarted (125 and 250) if conditions become dangerous. Usually, this means

if it starts raining during a race that started in the dry.

A 'Wet' race will not be stopped for changes in the weather. Any restarted race is automatically declared 'Wet' no matter what the conditions are. However, a 'Wet' race could still be stopped for overriding safety reasons.

The MotoGP race will not be interrupted for climatic reasons and riders who wish to change machine (when allowed), tyres or make adjustments must enter the pits and do so during the actual race. If the race is 'Wet', riders can change machines at any time. If the race is declared 'Dry', riders can only change machines after white flags have been displayed at all marshal posts.

If a Rider comes in on a machine with slick tyres he must go out on a bike with intermediate or wet tyres. Similarly, if he comes in on wets he must go out on slick or inters; and if he comes in on inters he must rejoin the race on slicks or wets.

A speed limit of 60kmh will be enforced in the pit lane. Overtaking is not permitted in the pit lane. Any rider who overtakes in the pit lane during a race will be penalised with a 'ride through'.

SCORING

Points are awarded from first to 15th place in all classes:

1st	25
2nd	20
3rd	16
4th	13
5th	12
6th	10
7th	9
8th	8
9th	7
10th	6
11th	5
12th	4
13th	3
14th	2
15th	1

If there is a tie in a race then the best lap time decides the place.

If riders are level on points in the Championship table then number of wins takes precedence, then the number of second places, and so on.

PENALTIES

The old ten second stop-and-go penalty for jumping the start or overtaking under a yellow flag has been replaced for 2004 by a new system.

The rider deemed to have infringed will be shown a yellow board with his number on it. He must enter pit lane within the next three laps and ride through without exceeding the 60kmh speed limit. If he doesn't respond within three laps he will be shown the black flag.

A yellow-flag infringement in qualifying will result in the time set on that lap being disregarded.

This is a minimum penalty. Race Direction can, if they consider the offence serious enough, award a time penalty, disqualify a rider, dock championship points, or ban him from subsequent events.

In the specific case of a yellow-flag offence during a race, a rider who realises his mistake can avoid punishment if he immediately raises his hand and lets the man he passed back through.

FLAGS

 TRACK CLEAR
Shown at every marshals' post during the first lap of every practice or qualifying session plus on sighting and warm-up laps. It will also be shown at individual marshals' posts after a yellow-flag incident has been cleared.

 DANGER AHEAD
Used to protect marshals and medics clearing a crash or debris. Riders must not overtake under yellow flags.

 OIL Shown motionless (not waved) to indicate rain, oil, cooling water, or other slippery substance on the track.

 CHANGE FROM 'DRY' TO 'WET' RACE
Shown when weather conditions change and informs riders in the MotoGP class only that they may now change bikes. New for this year.

 CHEQUERED FLAG
End of the race.

 DISQUALIFICATION
Shown with a rider's number to indicate they must immediately pull into the pits. Ignoring this one gets you in serious trouble.

It can be shown with an orange disc as well as a rider's number which tells him that his bike has a mechanical problem, for instance an oil leak, and he should get off the track immediately.

 RACE OR SESSION STOPPED
Used to interrupt the race, qualifying or practice and send the field back into pit lane. Usually seen for safety reasons, either a crash that needs clearing up or a change in the weather.

 LET FOLLOWING RIDER THROUGH
Used in qualifying to let a rider know there's another man coming up on a fast lap and in the race to tell a rider he is about to be lapped. You may also see it shown with the chequered flag if the leader is going to lap a rider close to the finish line.

BLUFFER'S GUIDE

Can't tell your swingarm from your IRTA? Our guide to the acronyms, abbreviations and codewords of the paddock will boost your banter

AGO – Giacomo Agostini, the most successful racer ever, with 123 GP victories, including eight 500cc and seven 350cc world titles. All were won with MV except the final 500 crown, which was achieved on a two-stroke Yamaha. By the way, his real friends call him Mino, not Ago.

AIRBOX – fed by air intakes with outlet(s) to engine inlet tract(s). Designed to be a plenum chamber, i.e. one that holds a volume of still air at a pressure slightly above atmospheric.

'BIG BANG' – describes an engine with close firing order.

BREMBO – Italian company that supplies most of the MotoGP grid with its carbon brakes.

CHATTER – low-amplitude pattering of a tyre, at typically 8Hz, the curse of tyre and suspension engineers. With patter the front tyre is trying hard to bounce on the track, thus lowering grip and reducing feel. It's very difficult to ride through.

CUT SLICK – not really a wet-weather tyre but often used on drying tracks. Designed to get some heat into the rubber as the tread blocks move about. If weather conditions are mixed, tyre technicians can often be seen cutting vestigial tread into a slick with modified soldering irons – hence 'cut slick'.

DELTABOX – Yamaha's trademark for the twin-spar aluminium frame design that has become the standard chassis layout for everyone except Ducati, who still use steel tube.

DESMODROMIC – system by which valves are positively opened and closed, effectively dispensing with the need for valve springs and allowing higher revs than with conventional springs. Only used by Ducati.

DORNA – the Spanish company that leases the rights to MotoGP from the FIM. They organise the calendar, negotiate with tracks and hold the commercial rights.

Read, learn and inwardly digest this bluffer's guide and you can put these two jokers – Julian Ryder and Toby Moody – out of a job. At the very least you'll be able to sound like you know what you're talking about

ELECTRICAL PROBLEM – catch-all excuse used by teams to explain any mechanical breakdown. Usually at least partially true, because when an engine lets go bits of flying red hot metal often cut through electrical wiring.

FIM – Fédération Internationale Motocycliste, the world-wide governing body of all motorcycle sport. Every country has its own constituent member of the FIM; in the UK it is the Auto Cycle Union (ACU). The FIM has an agreement for Dorna to run the commercial aspects of the MotoGP championship.

FIRING ORDER – the hot topic of last season. Refers to the intervals between each power impulse. On a normal four-cylinders-in-line motor there would be even gaps, one every 180 degrees of crank rotation. On a 'V' motor the intervals would depend on the angle of the 'V'. If the crank geometry is altered (the proper term is 'rephased') to move power impulses closer together the result is a 'big bang' engine.

FULL WET – a tyre designed for very wet conditions.

GRAND PRIX COMMISSION – the body that governs GPs. It is made up of Dorna CEO Carmelo Ezpeleta, Claude Danis of the FIM, Sito Pons in his capacity as president of IRTA and Takanao Tsubouchi, secretary of the MSMA. Race Director Paul Butler acts as secretary. This body deals with the rules, both technical and sporting, that govern GPs.

HIGHSIDE – a crash in which the rear tyre loses grip, usually under power, slides and then grips again. This has the effect of flicking the bike straight which catapults the rider out of the saddle. It's spectacular, scary and usually very painful.

HRC – Honda Racing Corporation, Honda's specialist competition arm. Runs the factory's road racing, motocross and trials teams. Only Honda factory team riders are HRC employees.

INTERMEDIATE – a wet-weather tyre that isn't as heavily treaded as a full wet but has more of a pattern than a cut slick.

IRTA – International Racing Teams Association, the organisation which contracts the teams to race, organises and polices the paddock, and runs the racing itself. Think of them as a supplier to Dorna.

KTM – an Austrian company, very successful in offroad and desert racing, supplying engines to Team KR this year.

LINKAGE – as in suspension link. The component that attaches to the rear suspension unit at one end and mounts on the swinging arm at the other. Two rods attach to the frame at one end and the centre of the link at the other. The relative geometry of the mounting points and the length of the rods define how the stiffness of the suspension changes with rear-wheel travel.

LOWSIDE – if you're going to crash a motorcycle, do it this way. Happens with the bike at big angles of lean when the tyres simply can't grip any more and the bike simply falls on its side.

MSMA – Motor Sports Manufacturers Association. The body that represents the manufacturers; Honda, Yamaha, Suzuki, Kawasaki, Ducati and Aprilia are members.

PNEUMATIC VALVES – using a reservoir of compressed air to close valves, standard practice in F1 but only used on Team Roberts's KTM motor in MotoGP. Allows higher revs than conventional springs.

PRO-LINK – Honda's rear suspension system (see Linkage). Suzuki used to call their system Full Floater, Kawasaki used Uni-Trak and Yamaha Monocross, but not any more.

PUSH – this can mean something as simple as trying harder, but usually refers to a rider taking liberties with front-tyre adhesion. (Listen for 'I was pushing the front' in post-race interviews.) Pushing too hard can result in washing and, perversely, can be brought on by good grip at the rear overpowering the front.

RACE DIRECTION – the four-man body that runs the races. The members are Paul Butler, the Race Director, Claude Danis of the FIM, IRTA safety delegate and 1982 500cc World Champion Franco Uncini, and Javier Alonso, representing Dorna. They make decisions, on a majority vote, on jump starts and other rule infringements. Disqualification of a rider needs a unanimous decision.

SET-UP – a wide-ranging term covering all the variables that can be altered from circuit to circuit, such as suspension settings, chassis geometry, and engine management software parameters.

SLICK – a treadless tyre used in dry conditions.

SLIPPER CLUTCH – essentially a freewheel device like the one that lets a bicycle freewheel downhill without the pedals going round. It limits the amount of engine braking force allowed to reach the rear wheel. This is varied from track to track and even from corner to corner, and is designed to keep a bike stable on the brakes and in corner entries.

SRT – Suter Racing Technology. The Swiss company, run by ex-250 privateer Eskil Suter, that designs and builds Kawasaki's frames.

SWINGING ARM – or swingarm, as the Yanks would say. This is the pivoted fork that holds the rear wheel's axle in its open end and pivots in the chassis at its closed end.

WASH – as in wash out. The result of pushing the front too hard and losing grip.

137

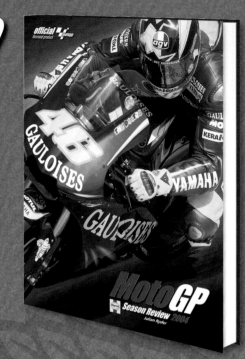

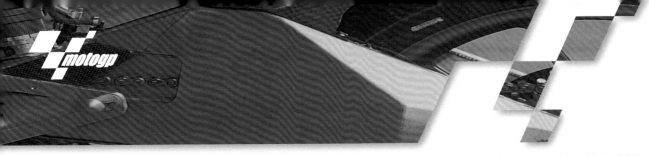

MotoGP STATS

A comprehensive range of facts and figures from the database of Dr Martin Raines, supplier to Dorna of MotoGP statictics

2004 MotoGP Championship

1	Rossi, Valentino	304	16	Hopkins, John	45
2	Gibernau, Sete	257	17	Hodgson, Neil	38
3	Biaggi, Max	217	18	Roberts, Kenny	37
4	Barros, Alex	165	19	McWilliams, Jeremy	26
5	Edwards, Colin	157	20	Byrne, Shane	18
6	Tamada, Makoto	150	21	Aoki, Nobuatsu	10
7	Checa, Carlos	117	22	Fabrizio, Michel	8
8	Hayden, Nicky	117	23	Kagayama, Yukio	7
9	Capirossi, Loris	117	24	Jacque, Olivier	5
10	Nakano, Shinya	83	25	Haydon, James	4
11	Xaus, Ruben	77	26	Ellison, James	3
12	Melandri, Marco	75	27	Pitt, Andrew	2
13	Abe, Norick	74	28	Ui, Youichi	1
14	Bayliss, Troy	71	29	Roberts, Kurtis	1
15	Hofmann, Alex	51			

500/MotoGP Champions

2004	Rossi	1976	Sheene
2003	Rossi	1975	Agostin
2002	Rossi	1974	Read
2001	Rossi	1973	Read
2000	Roberts Jnr	1972	Agostini
1999	Criville	1971	Agostini
1998	Doohan	1970	Agostini
1997	Doohan	1969	Agostini
1996	Doohan	1968	Agostini
1995	Doohan	1967	Agostini
1994	Doohan	1966	Agostini
1993	Schwantz	1965	Hailwood
1992	Rainey	1964	Hailwood
1991	Rainey	1963	Hailwood
1990	Rainey	1962	Hailwood
1989	Lawson	1961	Hocking
1988	Lawson	1960	Surtees
1987	Gardner	1959	Surtees
1986	Lawson	1958	Surtees
1985	Spencer	1957	Liberati
1984	Lawson	1956	Surtees
1983	Spence	1955	Duke
1982	Uncini	1954	Duke
1981	Lucchinelli	1953	Duke
1980	Roberts Snr	1952	Masetti
1979	Roberts Snr	1951	Duke
1978	Roberts Snr	1950	Masetti
1977	Sheene	1949	Graham

Grand Prix wins by Nation

		Total	MotoGP	500	350	250	125	80	50
1	Italy	641	35	135	66	182	202	3	18
2	Great Britain*	381		138	85	96	52	1	9
3	Spain	257	8	19	1	46	113	27	43
4	Germany**	171		1	11	81	44	6	28
5	USA	169		150		19			
6	Japan	158	3	9	8	57	75		6
7	Australia	127		84	14	16	10		3
8	Rhodesia***	70		12	31	23	4		
9	Switzerland	60		1	1	7	25	9	17
	France	60		3	9	33	15		
11	Holland	57		8		1	11		37
12	South Africa	39			21	18			
13	Venezuela	35		3	11	19	2		
14	New Zealand	31		3	2	1	17		8
15	Finland	24		3	11	10			

* Includes Northern Ireland
**Includes riders from the former East and West Germany
*** Now known as Zimbabwe

Tracks

	Track	Top Speed (mph)	Av. speed of lap record (mph)
Spain	Jerez de la Frontera	180.579	96.260
Portugal	Estoril	212.395	95.052
France	Le Mans	191.764	99.388
Italy	Mugello	213.140	105.578
Catalunya	Circuit de Catalunya	210.903	101.055
The Netherlands	Assen	196.425	112.852
Great Britain	Donington Park	177.099	100.026
Germany	Sachsenring	180.765	97.698
Czech Republic	Brno	193.380	101.312
Japan	Twin Ring Motegi	192.696	98.964
Malaysia	Sepang	197.419	100.696
Qatar	Losail	207.796	94.962
Australia	Phillip Island	205.062	109.222
Valencia	Circuito Ricardo Tormo	199.532	96.009

Winning Percentage in MotoGP/500cc class

	Rider	starts	wins	winning %
1	Valentino Rossi	80	42	52.5
2	Mick Doohan	137	54	39.4
3	Kenny Roberts (Snr)	58	22	37.9
4	Freddie Spencer	62	20	32.3
5	Wayne Rainey	83	24	28.9

Podium Appearance Percentage in MotoGP/500cc class

	Rider	starts	podiums	podium%
1	Valentino Rossi	80	65	81.2
2	Wayne Rainey	83	64	77.1
3	Mick Doohan	137	95	69.3
4	Kenny Roberts (Snr)	58	39	67.2
5	Eddie Lawson	127	78	61.4

Average Points per Start in MotoGP/500cc class

(adjusted to current scoring system)

	Rider	starts	points	pts/start
1	Valentino Rossi	80	1550	19.37
2	Mick Doohan	137	2399	17.51
3	Wayne Rainey	83	1443	17.39
4	Kenny Roberts (Snr)	58	995	17.16
5	Eddie Lawson	127	2018	15.89

Pole Position Percentage in MotoGP/500cc class

	Rider	starts	poles	pole%
1	Mick Doohan	137	58	42.3
2	Freddie Spencer	62	26	41.9
3	Johnny Cecotto	34	11	32.3
4	Valentine Rossi	80	25	31.2
5	Kenny Roberts (Snr)	58	18	31.0

Youngest riders to win the MotoGP/500cc Championship

	Rider	Age on winning Championship	Year
1	Freddie Spencer	21 years 258 days	1983
2	Mike Hailwood	22 years 160 days	1962
3	John Surtees	22 years 182 days	1956
4	Valentino Rossi	22 years 240 days	2001
5	Gary Hocking	23 years 316 days	1961

Youngest riders to win a MotoGP/500cc Grand Prix

	Rider	Age at first win	Race
1	Freddie Spencer	20 years 196 days	Belgium/1982/Spa
2	Norick Abe	20 years 227 days	Japan/1996/Suzuka
3	Randy Mamola	20 years 239 days	Belgium/1980/Zolder
4	Mike Hailwood	21 years 75 days	Britain/1961/IOM TT
5	Valentino Rossi	21 years 144 days	Britain/2000/Donington

Youngest riders to win the 250cc World Championship

In 2004 Dani Pedrosa became both the youngest ever rider to win the 250cc World Title having also become the youngest ever rider to win a 250cc Grand Prix at the first race of the year in South Africa.

	Rider	Age on winning Championship	Year
1	Dani Pedrosa	19 years 18 days	2004
2	Marco Melandri	20 years 74 days	2002
3	Valentino Rossi	20 years 250 days	1999
4	Manuel Poggiali	20 years 261 days	2003
5	Mike Hailwood	21 years 168 days	1961

Youngest riders to win a 250cc Grand Prix

	Rider	Age at first 250cc win	Race
1	Dani Pedrosa	18 years 202 days	South Africa/2004/Welkom
2	Alan Carter	18 years 227 days	France/1983/Le Mans
3	Marco Melandri	18 years 349 days	Germay/2001/Sachsenring
4	Johnny Cecotto	19 years 64 days	France/1975/Paul Ricard
5	Valentino Rossi	19 years 131 days	Dutch TT/1998/Assen

Youngest riders to win the 125cc World Championship

In 2004 Andrea Dovizioso became the fourth youngest rider ever to win the 125cc World Title.

	Rider	Age on winning Championship	Year
1	Loris Capirossi	17 years 165 days	1990
2	Dani Pedrosa	18 years 13 days	2003
3	Valentino Rossi	18 years 196 days	1997
4	Andrea Dovizioso	18 years 201 days	2004
5	Manuel Poggiali	18 years 262 days	2001

Youngest riders to win a 125cc Grand Prix

	Rider	Age	Race
1	Marco Melandri (Ita)	15 years 324 days	Dutch TT/1998/Assen/125cc
2	Jorge Lorenzo (Spa)	16 years 139 days	Rio/2003/Nelson Piquet/125cc
3	Ivan Goi (Ita)	16 years 157 days	Austria/1996/A1-Ring/125cc
4	Hector Barbera (Spa)	16 years 253 days	Britain/2003/Donington/125cc
5	Daniel Pedrosa (Spa)	16 years 273 days	Dutch TT/2002/Assen/125cc

Average age of Grand Prix podium finishers (years)

Year	MotoGP	250cc	125cc
2000	26.9	24.9	26.8
2001	27.3	25.8	23.7
2002	28.1	22.7	23.6
2003	28.6	22.5	22
2004	29.5	22.1	20.4

Number of wins in MotoGP/500cc class

Only Giacomo Agostini and Mick Doohan have won more GP races in the premier-class. Rossi needs 12 wins in 2005 to go level with Doohan in the following list.

68	Giacomo Agostini	25	Kevin Schwantz
54	Mick Doohan	24	Wayne Rainey
42	Valentino Rossi	22	Geoff Duke
37	Mike Hailwood		Kenny Roberts
31	Eddie Lawson		John Surtees

Number of premier class World Championship Titles

In 2005 Rossi could take his fifth title in the premier-class, the same number as Mick Doohan. Only Agostini with 8 World Titles has won more.

8	Giacomo Agostini (1966, 1967, 1968, 1969, 1970, 1971, 1972, 1975)
5	Mick Doohan (1994, 1995, 1996, 1997, 1998)
4	Valentino Rossi (2001, 2002, 2003, 2004)
	Geoff Duke (1951, 1953, 1954, 1955)
	Mike Hailwood (1962, 1963, 1964, 1965)
	Eddie Lawson (1984, 1986, 1988, 1989)
	John Surtees (1956, 1958, 1959, 1960)

Number of World Championship Titles (all solo classes)

Rossi could take his 7th World Title in 2005, the same number as Phil Read and John Surtees in the following list.

15	Giacomo Agostini (8 x 500cc, 7 x 350cc)
13	Angel Nieto (7 x 125cc, 6 x 50cc)
9	Mike Hailwood (4 x 500cc, 2 x 350cc, 3 x 250cc)
	Carlo Ubbiali (3 x 250cc, 6 x 125cc)
7	Phil Read (2 x 500cc, 4 x 250cc, 1 x 125cc)
	John Surtees (4 x 500cc, 3 x 350cc)
6	Valentino Rossi (3 x MotoGP, 1 x 500cc, 1 x 250cc, 1 x 125cc)
	Geoff Duke (4 x 500cc, 2 x 350cc)
	Jim Redman (4 x 350cc, 2 x 250cc)

All-time podium finishes in all solo classes of GP racing

Rossi has scored 101 podium finishes in all classes of GP racing, six less than his great rival Max Biaggi. Both Rossi and Biaggi could move above Mike Hailwood in this list during 2005.

	Rider	Total podium finishes	Wins	Seconds	Thirds
1	Giacomo Agostini	159	122	35	2
2	Angel Nieto	139	90	35	14
3	Phil Read	121	52	44	25
4	Mike Hailwood	112	76	25	11
5	Max Biaggi	107	42	39	26
6	Valentino Rossi	101	68	21	12
7	Jim Redman	98	45	33	20
8	Mick Doohan	95	54	31	10
9	Luigi Taveri	89	30	33	26
10	Anton Mang	84	42	25	17

Podium finishes in the premier class of GP racing

In the premier class Rossi is already 4th in the all-time list of podium finishers and could go to third place in this table above Eddie Lawson with 14 top-three finishes in 2005.

	Rider	Total podium finishes	Wins	Seconds	Thirds
1	Mick Doohan	95	54	31	10
2	Giacomo Agostini	88	68	20	0
3	Eddie Lawson	78	31	31	16
4	Valentino Rossi	65	42	15	8
5	Wayne Rainey	64	24	22	18
6	Randy Mamola	54	13	22	19
	Max Biaggi	54	13	24	17
8	Wayne Gardner	52	18	20	14
9	Kevin Schwantz	51	25	13	13
	Alex Criville	51	15	16	20
11	Mike Hailwood	48	37	9	2
12	Barry Sheene	40	19	10	11
13	Kenny Roberts	39	22	12	5
14	Phil Read	34	11	13	10
15	Geoff Duke	32	22	5	5

All-time Grand Prix wins – all solo classes

Only three riders have scored more GP victories (in all solo-classes) than Valentino Rossi. Eight victories during 2005 could take him to 76 GP victories, the same as Mike Hailwood.

	Rider	Total Wins	World Titles	MotoGP/500cc	350cc	250cc	125cc	80/50cc
1	Giacomo Agostini	122	15	68	54			
2	Angel Nieto	90	13				62	28
3	Mike Hailwood	76	9	37	16	21	2	
4	Valentino Rossi	68	6	42		14	12	
5	Mick Doohan	54	5	54				
6	Phil Read	52	7	11	4	27	10	
7	Jim Redman	45	6	2	21	18	4	
8	Anton Mang	42	5		8	33	1	
	Max Biaggi	42	4	13		29		
10	Carlo Ubbiali	39	9			13	26	
11	John Surtees	38	7	22	15	1		
12	Jorge Martinez	37	4				15	22
13	Luca Cadalora	34	3	8		22	4	
14	Geoff Duke	33	6	22	11			
15	Kork Ballington	31	4			14	17	
	Eddie Lawson	31	4	31				
17	Luigi Taveri	30	3			2	22	6
18	Pierpaolo Bianchi	27	3				24	3
	Eugenio Lazzarini	27	3				9	18
	Freddie Spencer	27	3	20		7		

Top Grand Prix wins by Manufacturer – all solo classes

Honda, who became the first manufacturer to take 500 Grand Prix victories when Valentino Rossi won the 500cc race at the Japanese GP in 2001, could reach the milestone 600th GP victory in 2005.

		Total	MotoGP	500	350	250	125	80	50
1	Honda	587	36	156	35	188	159		13
2	Yamaha	411	11	120	68	165	47		
3	MV-Agusta	274		139	75	26	34		
4	Aprilia	177				102	75		
5	Suzuki	154		89			35		30
6	Kawasaki	85		2	28	45	10		
	Derbi	85				1	42	25	17
8	Kreidler	72							72
9	Garelli	51					44		7
10	Gilera	47		35	4		8		
11	Moto Guzzi	45		3	24	18			
12	Norton	41		21	20				
13	Morbidelli	35				5	30		
14	Minarelli	32					32		
15	Harley Davidson	28			4	24			
	Bultaco	28				1	6		21
17	MBA	23				1	22		
18	NSU	20				12	8		
19	Mondial	18				4	14		
20	Benelli	13				13			
	MZ	13			1	7	5		
	Krauser	13						13	

WIN GREAT PRIZES

■ Paddock passes for Donington MotoGP 2005
■ Books signed by MotoGP stars

We have fantastic prizes to give away to six of you enthusiasts who've made the very wise choice to buy a copy of *MotoGP Season Guide 2005* – the MotoGP fan's essential companion to the action-packed 2005 season. All you have to do is answer a simple question by using your own knowledge or finding the answer within this book.

THE QUESTION
At Donington, what's the name of the first corner after the start/finish line?

THE PRIZES
■ Two paddock passes for the Donington MotoGP round on July 22-24.
■ A unique copy of the highly acclaimed *MotoGP Season Review 2004* signed on the front cover by Valentino Rossi.
■ Four more special signed copies of the *MotoGP Season Review 2004* from Max Biaggi, Sete Gibernau, Nicky Hayden and Shinya Nakano – each of these is a 'custom' version with a unique cover and a genuine signature in silver ink.

HOW TO ENTER
Write your answer on a postcard or on the back of a sealed envelope with your name and address and send it to:

MotoGP Season Guide 2005 Competition
Haynes Publishing (SIPD)
Sparkford
Yeovil
Somerset BA22 7JJ